Alternate Light Source Imaging

Alternate Light Source Imaging

Forensic Photography Techniques

Norman Marin

Jeffrey Buszka

Series Editor

Larry S. Miller

Routledge
Taylor & Francis Group
LONDON AND NEW YORK

First published 2013 by Anderson publishing

Published 2015 by Routledge
2 Park Square, Milton Park, Abingdon, Oxon OX14 4RN

and by Routledge
711 Third Avenue, New York, NY 10017, USA

Routledge is an imprint of the Taylor & Francis Group, an informa business

British Library Cataloguing-in-Publication Data
A catalogue record for this book is available from the British Library

Library of Congress Cataloging-in-Publication Data
A catalog record for this book is available from the Library of Congress

ISBN 978-1-4557-7762-4 (pbk)

CONTENTS

CHAPTER 1

Electromagnetic Radiation

Photography allows the forensic scientist and crime scene investigator the means by which to document the scene and articles of evidence that may be presented before a judge and jury. Frequently, physical evidence must be discovered using tunable wavelength light sources. Trace evidence, fingerprints, body fluids, and other forms of evidence may be discovered using light sources that emit radiation ranging from the ultraviolet (UV) to the infrared (IR) spectrum. The photographer must be able to successfully capture an image of this evidence using the same light source. In order to learn how to capture images using alternate light sources, the photographer must understand the medium, light, and how it relates to the camera.

The interaction between light (or electromagnetic radiation) and matter has been scientifically studied and used to both characterize and identify substances. The advancement of this science is best seen in the field of analytical spectroscopy where very small quantities of an analyte can be exposed to electromagnetic radiation. The manner in which an analyte responds to radiation may be characteristic of a known substance. The examination of evidence with the use of an alternate light source is similar. The physical properties of evidence or the surface on which evidence may reside can facilitate the reflectance, transmission, and absorption of light. Furthermore, the absorption of light by a substance may result in fluorescence or phosphorescence, instances where the substance reemits light. When using light to examine physical evidence, it is of course important to understand the nature of light and how it may interact with a substance. With this knowledge, the characteristic properties of a forensic sample can be recognized and documented. In this chapter, the electromagnetic spectrum and properties of light will be discussed.

1.1 LIGHT AND THE ELECTROMAGNETIC SPECTRUM

Electromagnetic radiation is a radiant energy that exhibits wave-like motion as it travels through space. Everyday examples of electromagnetic radiation include the light from the sun; the energy to cook food

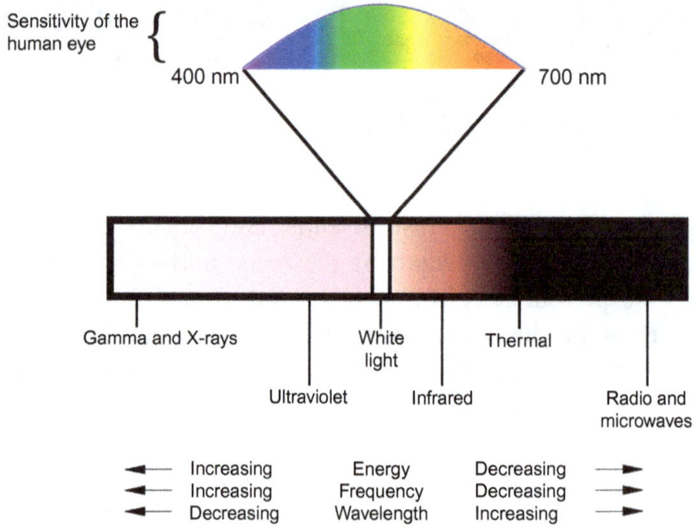

Figure 1.1 The electromagnetic spectrum is the distribution of all electromagnetic waves arranged according to frequency and wavelength.

in a microwave; X-rays used by doctors to visualize the internal structures of the body; radio waves used to transmit a signal to the television or radio; and the radiant heat from a fireplace.

Electromagnetic radiation can be divided into several categories that include gamma and X-rays, UV radiation, visible light, IR radiation, thermal radiation, radio waves, and microwaves. When electromagnetic radiation is categorized according to wavelength, it is referred to as the electromagnetic spectrum (Figure 1.1).

Visible light or white light comprises the individual colors of the rainbow. This is evident when light passes through a prism and is separated into its component colors. The different colors correspond to different wavelengths and frequencies of visible electromagnetic radiation. Red light has a longer wavelength, lower frequency, and lesser energy than blue light. The order of the visible light spectrum based on increasing wavelength and decreasing energy is violet, indigo, blue, green, yellow, orange, and red (Figure 1.2).

Visible light comprises only a small portion of the electromagnetic spectrum, but it is the only part that humans can perceive without the aid of a detector. Our eyes are most sensitive to green light. Digital cameras have sensor elements that are designed to mimic how we

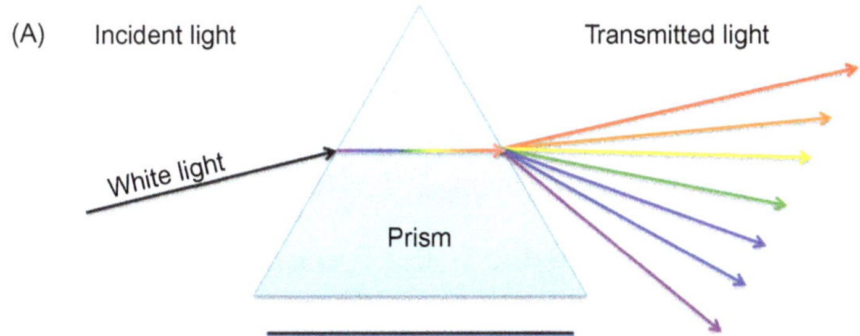

Color	Wavelength
Red	620–700 nm
Orange	590–620 nm
Yellow	575–590 nm
Green	490–575 nm
Blue	430–490 nm
Violet	400–430 nm

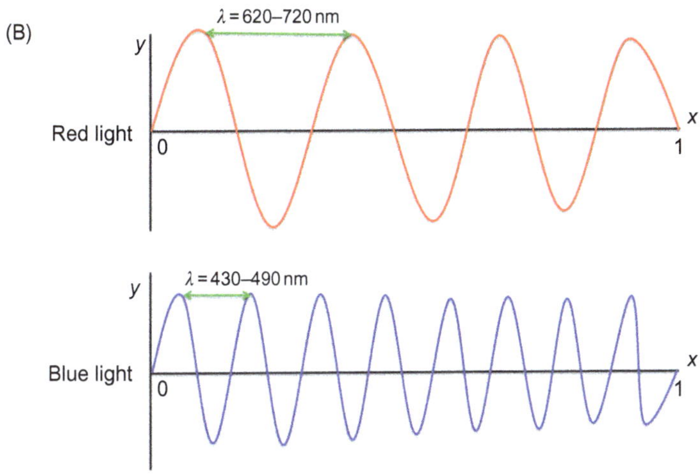

Figure 1.2 (A) As white light passes through a prism, it is refracted or bent and consequently separates into its component colors. Red light having the longest wavelength deviates the least from the original path of light, whereas blue light refracts the most. (B) Red light will have a longer wavelength than blue light. As implied in Eq. (1.1), there is an inverse relationship between frequency and wavelength. In this graphical example, it can be seen that the shorter the distance between waves,the greater is the frequency increase with a given distance and period of time.

perceive colors. For example, in a camera that possesses a Bayer filter over its sensor, there are typically twice as many green filters as there are blue and red. The imaging sensors used in digital cameras are also sensitive to UV and IR radiation. However, in order to take advantage of the full sensitivity to UV and IR radiation, the camera needs to be stripped of its internal filters.

The term *infrared* refers to a broad range of wavelengths, starting from just beyond red to the start of those frequencies used for communication. The wavelength range is from about 700 nm up to 1 mm. The region adjacent to the visible spectrum is called the "near-IR," and the longer wavelength region is called "far-IR."

The region just below the visible spectrum in is called the *ultraviolet*. The wavelength range is from about 10 to 400 nm. Ultraviolet means the part of the electromagnetic spectrum that is shorter in wavelength than the color violet. The region adjacent to the visible spectrum is called the "near-UV." Most solid substances absorb UV very strongly.

1.2 PROPERTIES OF LIGHT

As light propagates through space, it exhibits wave-like motion. Waves have three primary characteristics: wavelength, frequency, and speed (Figure 1.3). In a vacuum, all electromagnetic radiation travels at the same speed, the "speed of light," which is approximately 2.9979×10^8 m/s. A wavelength can be defined as the distance between two consecutive peaks or valleys in a wave. Frequency is the number

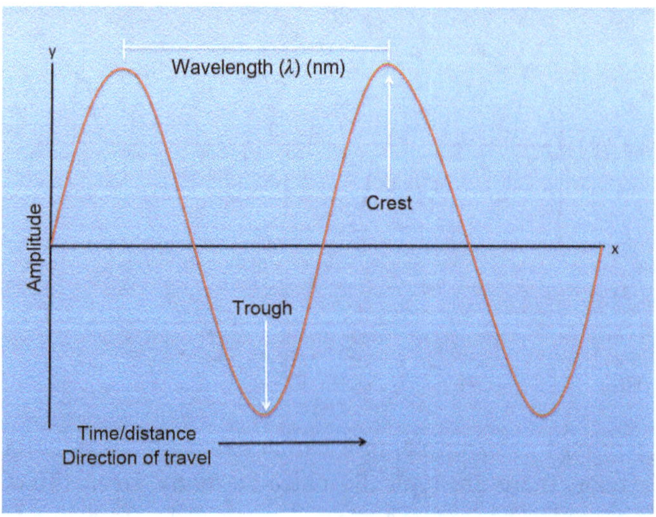

Figure 1.3 The properties of waves include wavelength, frequency, and speed. The wavelength is typically represented by the Greek letter lambda (λ) and is the distance between wave crests measured in nanometers (nm). The wavelength represents one complete cycle of a wave. The frequency of a wave is the number of crests that occur within a given period of time, and the speed of the wave is the distance that it travels per unit time.

of waves that pass a single point in a given period of time. Speed, frequency, and wavelength are related by the equation:

$$\lambda\nu = c \tag{1.1}$$

where

c = the speed of light (m/s)
ν = frequency (1/s)
λ = wavelength (m)

There is an inverse relationship between frequency and wavelength. Short wavelength radiation has a high frequency. The wave with the longest wavelength will have the lowest frequency. Throughout this chapter, we will be describing several different types of electromagnetic radiation and the tools used to detect and photograph the radiation. The convention that will be used to characterize the radiation will be wavelength, using distance units of nanometers (nm). A nanometer is a unit of distance measurement that is equivalent to 1 billionth of a meter. In forensic photography there are three areas of the electromagnetic spectrum that can be imaged with silicon sensor based digital SLR cameras. The near-ultraviolet region of the electromagnetic spectrum ranges between 300 and 400 nm, the visible region between 400 and 700 nm, and the near-IR region from 700 to 1100 nm.

1.3 LIGHT AND MATTER

When electromagnetic radiation is incident on matter, the radiation can be reflected, transmitted, absorbed, or a combination of the three. Understanding how radiation interacts with matter and how wavelength selection can be used to enhance evidentiary material is the basis for forensic photography.

Reflection occurs when light is incident onto an object and it bounces or is reflected. The light reflected could be characterized as specular reflection or a diffuse reflection. Specular reflection occurs when light is reflected from a flat or smooth surface. In a specular reflection, the angle of incidence is equal to the angle of reflection, and the reflected rays are parallel. Diffuse reflection occurs with textured surfaces. The incident illumination is diffused or scattered in many directions from the surface of the object (Figure 1.4).

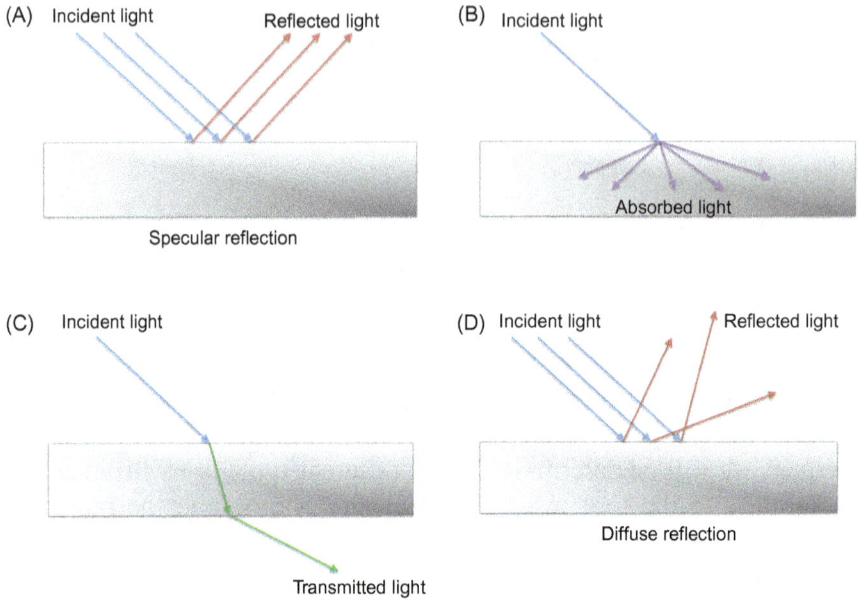

Figure 1.4 Radiation can be (A) reflected, (B) absorbed, or (C) transmitted by an object. In specular reflection, the reflected rays are typically parallel to each other. Diffuse reflection (D) differs from specular reflection (A) in that the reflected rays are not parallel due to the nonuniform surface.

When white light reaches the surface of an object, the object can absorb some or all of the incident illumination. If the object absorbs all of the radiation, it will appear black. If the object reflects all the illumination, it appears white. When an object absorbs light, the light energy is converted into heat energy. This is why it is not recommended to wear dark colored clothing on a hot summer day. Dark clothes will absorb the light and transform the electromagnetic radiation into heat energy, whereas light colored clothes will reflect much of the light.

On a molecular level, when an object absorbs the incident illumination, a portion of the object's molecular structure is promoted to an electronically excited state. When it is in an excited state, several things can happen: the energy may be transformed into heat energy, or luminescence may occur. Luminescence is the release of radiation by a molecule, or an atom, after it has absorbed energy and has been promoted to an excited (higher energy) state. The two most apparent types of luminescence are fluorescence and phosphorescence.

When light is not absorbed or reflected by the molecular composition of an object, it passes through the object or is transmitted. Glass

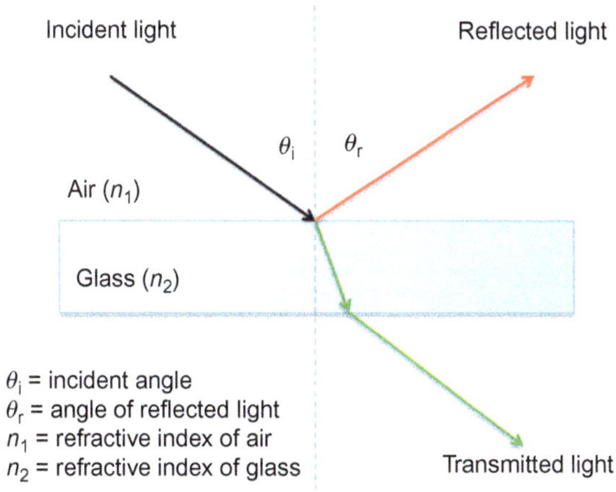

Figure 1.5 Some materials will reflect and transmit light simultaneously. However, as light travels from one medium to another (e.g., from air into glass) the direction, speed, and wavelength of the light can change. In this image, a portion of the incident ray is reflected while the portion transmitted undergoes refraction as it enters the glass from the air and again as it exits the glass and reenters the air. As light travels into a medium of a higher refractive index, it will bend toward the normal. As it travels from a material with a higher refractive index to a lesser one, light will bend away from the normal.

and water are everyday examples of materials that facilitate the transmission of light. These materials, however, may also reflect light as well as bend or refract light (Figure 1.5). As light passes from one medium into another (e.g., from air into water), the changes in refractive index between the two mediums may cause light rays to change their speed and their direction of travel. The degree to which a material bends light is termed its refractive index. Additionally, while the frequency of light does not change as it passes into a different medium, its wavelength does change. The controlled ability to change the wavelength of light through transmission is the basis for light filtration.

1.4 LUMINESCENCE

British scientist Sir George G. Stokes coined the term fluorescence in the 1850s. Stokes made the observation that the mineral fluorspar emitted light when illuminated with UV radiation. Stokes observed that the fluorescing light was longer in wavelength than the excitation (incident) radiation. This phenomenon became known as the Stokes shift (Figure 1.6).

If the emission of light persists for up to a few seconds after the excitation radiation is discontinued, the process is known as

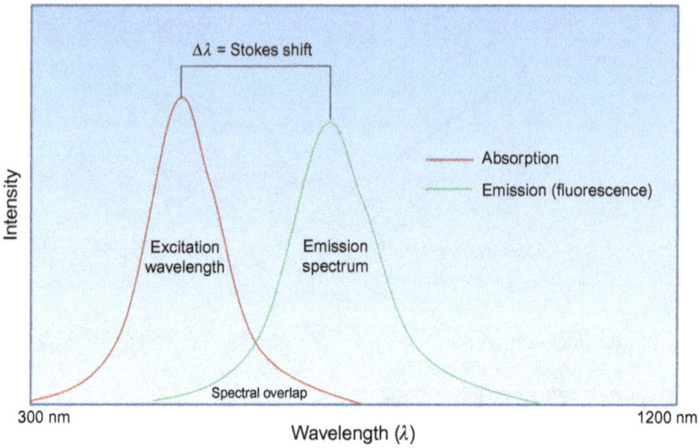

Figure 1.6 A fluorescent material will absorb light and reemit it at a longer wavelength. This phenomenon is referred to as a Stokes shift.

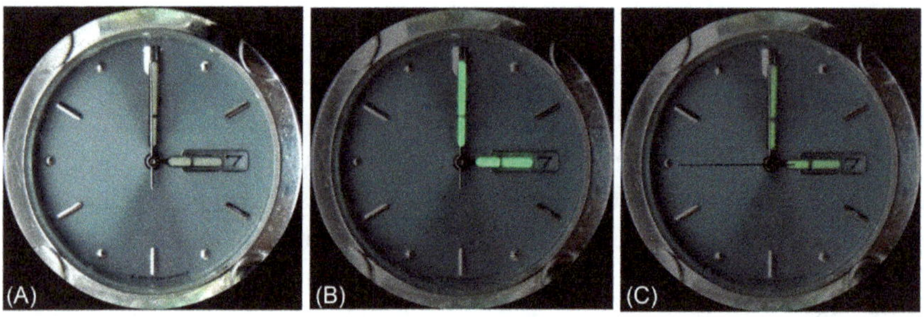

Figure 1.7 (A) Normal flash photography. (B) Time 0, immediately after the lights were turned off. (C) Approximately 45 seconds after the lights were turned off. Images (B) and (C) were recorded in a darkened room where the camera was mounted on a tripod. The exposure settings were f5.0, 1/3 seconds, and ISO 200.

phosphorescence. Fluorescence is observed only after the immediate absorption of the excitation radiation. The fluorescence emission of radiation typically has an average lifetime of 10^{-5}–10^{-8} seconds (about 1 millionth of a second). The average lifetime of phosphorescence may range from 10^{-4} to several seconds.

An example of phosphorescence can be found in the painted hands of a wristwatch. The hands are painted with phosphorescent ink, which absorbs light when illuminated and then reemits light at a longer wavelength over a period of time.

In Figure 1.7A, the image of the watch face was taken using normal flash photography. The image in Figure 1.7B was recorded immediately after the lights were turned off; the hands phosphoresced brightly. The image in Figure 1.7C was recorded approximately 45 seconds later when the phosphorescence had diminished. This is in contrast to fluorescence where the fluorescent emission ceases almost immediately after excitation radiation is discontinued.

Incandescence occurs when light is emitted from an object as a result of heating. Molten rock, glass, or metals are examples of materials that may undergo incandescence when heated. In this context, the term "glow" can be associated with incandescence. Luminescent reactions are not caused by the addition of heat; this distinguishes luminescence from incandescence. It is not unusual for fluorescence to be erroneously referred to or described as a "glowing" reaction. The circumstances under which objects "glow" or incandesce are not the same for luminescence. Similarly, "glow sticks" are misleadingly named. Light emission from these objects is the result of a chemical reaction or chemiluminescence.

Luminescence can be induced in a wide variety of forensic samples to help locate, identify, and quantitatively analyze evidence. For example,

- Fibers
- Gunshot residue
- Biological fluids
  - Semen
  - Saliva
  - Vaginal secretions
  - Urine
  - Sweat
  - Decomposition fluid
- Pigments and inks
- Fingerprint development powders or dyes
- Petroleum products.

All these materials may luminesce under the right conditions when examined under light at specific wavelengths. However, to fully take advantage of these visualization methods requires further study regarding light filtration for the proper isolation of Stokes shift light. Additionally, the documentation aspects require study of the photographic techniques that could be used in combination with proper filtration.

CHAPTER 2

Photographic Equipment for Alternate Light Source Imaging

There are a myriad of equipment considerations to take into account when imaging evidence in a forensic setting. This section will focus on some of the aspects of digital imaging that the photographer must be aware of in order to capture high quality images and the equipment necessary to achieve this. Good photography, however, is ultimately predicated on the photographer's knowledge of the camera equipment and advanced camera operation. The photographer must know the equipment thoroughly, not only to use it properly but also to understand its limitations. Additionally, the photographer must understand the nature of the evidence being documented. Is the evidence a latent fingerprint enhanced with a fluorescent powder? Is it a ligature mark that shows contrast under UV radiation? How will this photograph be used? Is photography being performed to document what you see during an examination or will it be compared to some exemplar? The answers to these questions will certainly vary, but they will also dictate the file format and type of lens, camera, and other equipment that is used during photo documentation.

2.1 THE DIGITAL CAMERA AND ALTERNATE LIGHT PHOTOGRAPHY

Digital single lens reflex (DSLR) cameras are the preferred cameras for any work performed with a tunable wavelength light source. Compared to point and shoot cameras, DSLRs offer a full battery of adjustable user setting, from a fully programmed setting where the camera determines its shutter speed and aperture, to fully manual where the photographer dictates all the exposure settings. The wide array of available lenses coupled with the ability to change lenses on the fly makes these cameras quite adaptable. Various file formats are typically available in DSLR cameras whereas a point and shoot camera may only have the joint photographic experts group (JPEG) format available. The file format that is chosen by the photographer can have considerable effects on the resulting image. How the image can be developed in post-processing software and any limitations therein is also affected by the file format chosen. In this chapter, we will review camera equipment that is typically used in the documentation of evidence visualized with a tunable wavelength light source.

Until recently, film single lens reflex (SLR) cameras had been in manufacture for many years and had been considered the staple of any professional setup. However, these cameras are not as practical for work with alternate lighting systems. This is largely because film that is sensitive to infrared (IR) or ultraviolet (UV) radiation requires long exposure times and there was no guarantee the photography was successful until the film was developed. That has changed dramatically with the introduction of digital imaging with silicon-based sensors, prompting the elimination of film cameras.

An important component of the camera that should be understood as it relates to alternate light photography is the sensor. The sensor is located behind the focusing mirror and is generally blocked from view by the shutter. The sensor in most cameras that are manufactured for commercial use also have a filter positioned between the sensor and the lens elements that is commonly referred to as the "hot mirror." The hot mirror serves several purposes; it acts as a protective barrier between the actual sensor and the internal compartment of the camera. The hot mirror as a physical barrier between the sensor and the rest of the camera is beneficial because as lenses are changed, or if the camera is left exposed to the environment, it is inevitable that dust and debris will enter the camera. As a photograph is being taken, the sensor becomes electrically charged and can attract dust. If dust adheres to the sensor it may manifest in an image as dark spots.

The hot mirror also serves to block certain wavelengths of light that may lead to commercially unappealing photographs (Figure 2.1). If we look at a typical transmission spectrum for a hot mirror, we will see that radiation in the UV (350 nm and below) and the IR (750 nm and above) are blocked to some degree by the filter (Figure 2.2). The extent to which UV and IR radiations are blocked by the sensor can vary. Older DSLR cameras tend to have hot mirrors that allow more UV and/or IR radiation into the sensor than do those in newer camera models.

Removal of the hot mirror from the sensor is often required, to allow the camera to capture radiation in UV and IR wavelengths that

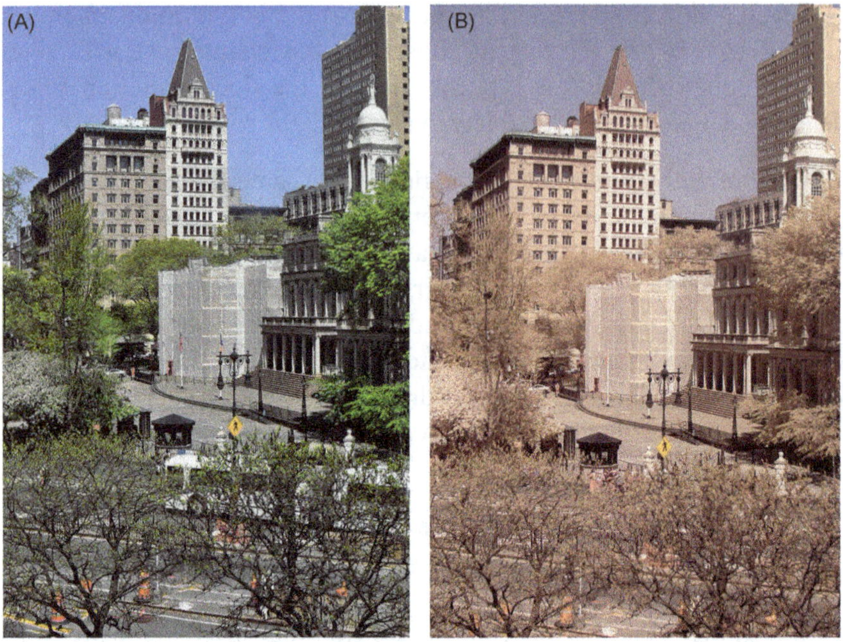

Figure 2.1 (A) The photograph was captured with an unmodified Nikon D90 camera. The hot mirror mostly allows light in the visible spectrum to reach the sensor so that color accuracy is maintained. (B) The photograph was captured with a Fuji S3 Pro full-spectrum camera. With the hot mirror removed, radiation across the full sensitivity of the sensor is captured. Since silicon sensors are more sensitive in the IR spectrum, the red channel tends to become over saturated resulting in the reddish hue to the overall image.

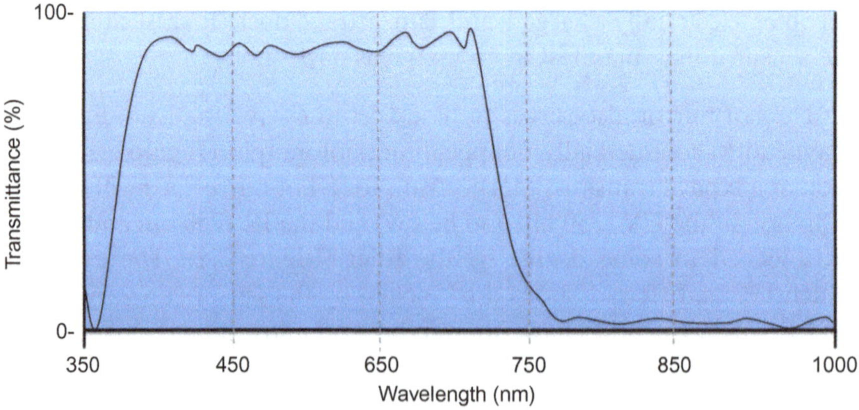

Figure 2.2 An example of a transmission spectrum of a hot mirror. The filter that is normally placed in front of the camera sensor serves to block light in the UV and IR spectrum while allowing visible light to reach the sensor.

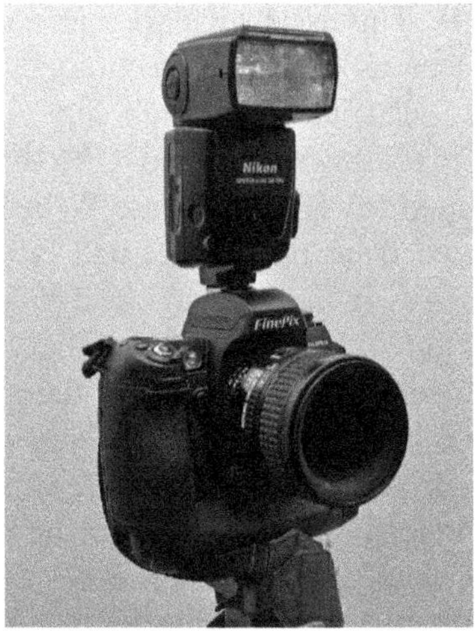

Figure 2.3 A Fuji S3 FinePix Pro IRUV DSLR camera equipped with a Nikon 60 mm macro lens and a Nikon SB-800 flash unit. This camera was manufactured by Fuji as a full-spectrum camera specifically for forensic applications but has since been discontinued.

are useful in forensic imaging. Cameras that do not have a hot mirror are typically referred to as full-spectrum cameras. At the time of this publication (2013), there are no cameras that are commercially manufactured in this manner. Fujifilm did manufacture a DSLR with the hot mirror removed for a period of time. This camera, the Fuji S3 FinePix Pro IRUV, was marketed mainly to law enforcement agencies. Unfortunately, Fuji stopped production of this camera despite the fact that the forensic applications of these cameras are indispensible (Figure 2.3).

Artistic photographers have explored the use of full-spectrum cameras for imaging landscapes and other subjects in the UV and IR spectrum. The demand for full-spectrum cameras created by these photographers has resulted in several after-market commercial services that will professionally remove the hot mirror and replace it with either a glass or an IR transmitting filter for a fee. A simple on-line search should yield various companies that perform these conversions however; careful research should be made as to the quality practices of after market full-spectrum conversion services. If you choose to modify a camera such that it can be used for full-spectrum imaging, there are several factors to consider when selecting a camera for conversion. The camera selected should be capable of generating a live preview, meaning that the subject can be previewed on the rear liquid crystal display (LCD). This is particularly necessary for IR imaging. The filters over the lens used with IR techniques are opaque and the subject cannot be visualized through the camera viewfinder. Additionally, when imaging with IR and UV, there is a focus shift if the lens is not calibrated for IR or UV use. When imaging with white light, the light reflected from the subject will fall on the plane of the sensor. If the same focus is maintained but the subject is illuminated with UV radiation, the radiation entering the camera will come to focus in front of the sensor. Conversely, if the subject is illuminated with IR radiation, the image will come to focus past the plane of the sensor. If efforts to correct the focus shift are not taken, the resulting images will appear blurred. While lenses can be calibrated for proper focusing, the live preview function makes focus corrections much simpler. Given focus shift, the camera selected for full-spectrum conversion should also be capable of manual focus control, a feature that is typically not available in point and shoot cameras. The imaging conditions in forensic settings, particularly with UV or narrowband visible light photography, usually require a darkened environment to prevent ambient light contamination. The auto-focus features in most cameras will not operate properly in darkened conditions, requiring the ability to manually focus the lens.

A candidate camera for full-spectrum conversion should also be capable of an aperture priority mode. Aperture priority allows the photographer to control the diameter of the lens aperture, which can directly affect both the amount of light that enters the camera and the range of distances along the axis of the lens that are in focus (also referred to as depth of field). There is an inverse relationship between these two parameters. If the diameter of the lens aperture is reduced, the depth of field increases, but less light enters the camera (Figure 2.4). Imaging subjects with IR and UV radiation, the aperture control can be used to control the exposure of the photograph and can compensate for focus shift.

2.2 LIGHT INTERPRETATION

As the shutter of a camera is released, the sensor is exposed to electromagnetic radiation that is transmitted through the lens elements and any filters placed before the sensor. The sensor records the intensity of radiation for the duration that the shutter is left open.

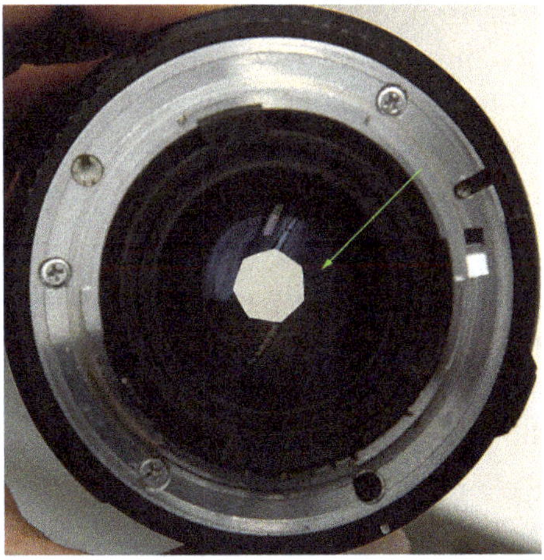

Figure 2.4 This image depicts the aperture diaphragm of a lens, highlighted by the green arrow. The diameter of the diaphragm is controlled by the "f" setting or "f-stop" selected by the photographer. Low f-numbers correspond to a wider aperture opening that allows more light into the camera. Conversely, high f-numbers correspond to smaller aperture diameters, which let less light into the camera. In addition to light control, the aperture diaphragm also controls depth of field in an image.

The sensor allows for the influx of photons to be converted into an electrical charge. The camera processor interprets the electrical charge captured and converts what is essentially analog data into a digitized format. Each image pixel generated represents a certain color, tone, and intensity that was inherent in the subject being photographed. The important thing to note here is that the resulting image is an interpretation of the electromagnetic radiation recorded by the camera.

Modern digital camera sensors are silicon based and have been shown to have sensitivity to light spanning wavelengths from 300 to 1000 nm of the electromagnetic spectrum. As previously mentioned, the hot mirror essentially blocks out radiation in the UV and IR spectrum so that the sensor predominantly records light in the visible spectrum. Furthermore, most cameras also have what is referred to as a Bayer filter in front of the image sensor. The Bayer filter allows light only in the red, blue, and green spectrum to pass through to the sensor. The resulting image is therefore a software generated combination of these colors, such that the original colors of the subject are reproduced. The process by which this occurs is referred to as Bayer interpolation. The algorithm used in the Bayer process is ultimately responsible for how the resultant image appears in terms of color, tone, hue, and saturation. This aspect of image formation is particularly important to understand when photographs are taken using radiation that is outside of the visible spectrum. When a camera is converted to full spectrum, the hot mirror is removed; however, the Bayer filter remains in the camera.

In the case of imaging in the IR spectrum, recall that IR radiation is not visible to the naked eye. Depending on the camera/filter combination being used, and white balancing, the camera processor will generally interpret an approximate color value for the wavelengths that are detected by the sensor which are not in the visible spectrum. For this reason, images captured with IR radiation are often referred to as "false color" photographs since these images do not actually represent the colors of the subject. Rather, the resulting image is a representation of radiation absorbed and reflected from the subject that is detected by the camera sensor.

2.3 CAMERA FILE FORMATS

The most common file format is the JPEG format. At the time of writing, this format is available virtually in every digital camera; however, it is also the least suitable format for evidence imaging. In order to appreciate why JPEG is not suitable, it is important to understand some basic information about file compression and decompression, juxtaposed with other file formats.

JPEG is a compressed image file format that is also referred to as a "lossy compression" format. In order to reduce the size of the image file, the camera processor deletes pixels (permanently) from the image. The benefit of this is a smaller file size, which allows for a faster write time from the camera's memory buffer to the memory card. A smaller file size also means you can store more images on the memory card versus other formats. The downside of this is the effects generated when the compressed file is decompressed by image-viewing software.

When a JPEG image file is opened, there are portions of the pixel data missing because of the compression process. During decompression, image-viewing software will run an algorithm to restore deleted pixels based on the color and luminous intensity of the non-deleted or neighboring pixels. This interpolation process typically results in what are referred to as decompression artifacts or pixilation, and consequently a loss in image resolution. Loss of image detail may not be readily identifiable, but it becomes apparent when one zooms into a portion of a photograph. If an image is taken for the purpose of comparison in JPEG format (such as a fingerprint or tool mark), it is likely that a loss of resolution will occur in the photo possibly preventing a comparison.

Image resolution refers to the amount of detail that can be seen in a digital image. The level of resolution loss in the JPEG format is commensurate with the level of image compression. A highly compressed JPEG image will result in a higher degree of resolution loss. A JPEG using less compression will generally result in less of a loss in resolution (Figure 2.5).

Additional formats to consider include TIFF (tagged image file format) and RAW. TIFF utilizes a lossless compression algorithm, meaning that the file is generated in such a manner that it retains all the data necessary to redisplay the original image. RAW, by contrast, does not typically utilize any file compression; lossless RAW formats are available in most high-end DSLR cameras. The drawback to these formats is the resulting file size of the image. TIFF and RAW images

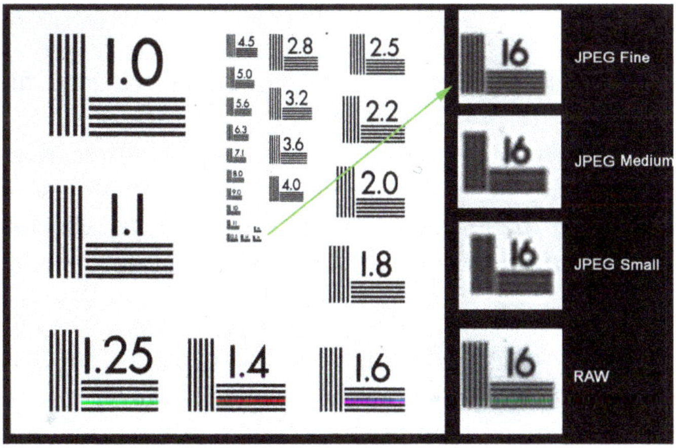

Figure 2.5 The left image is of a resolution test chart captured with a DSLR camera using a macro lens. The image was captured using a RAW format, and then three additional images were captured using JPEG with varying degrees of compression. As indicated by the green arrow, the images on the right demonstrate the extent of resolution loss as a function of compression on a magnified area of the test chart. The artifacts resulting from compression can be compared to the uncompressed RAW image.

can be large files, thereby decreasing storage capabilities and processing time.

It is considered best practice to photograph items of evidence with a non-compressed or lossless compression format. Most high-end DSLR cameras can save two formats simultaneously, such as JPEG and RAW whereby the JPEG can be utilized as a quick-viewing image while the RAW can be retained for post-processing and image development.

2.4 ISO AND LONG EXPOSURES

As imaging technology progresses, many digital camera manufacturers are pushing the upper limits of ISO capabilities in digital cameras. ISO is essentially the effective film speed of a digital camera and refers to the light gathering capabilities of the sensor. High ISO settings can be very useful, particularly in ALS photography, because in some cases photographs must be taken in complete darkness with a filter over the camera lens. This naturally prolongs the time required to capture a balanced exposure. While this may not be in an issue in the photography of still evidence, when photographing live victims of violent incidents using ALS techniques, prolonged exposures are not practical. Exposures that are longer than 1/60 of a second will require the camera and subject to be motionless otherwise the resulting photographs will appear blurred.

Increasing the ISO number on the digital camera makes the sensor more light sensitive. This can result in shorter exposure times but often at the cost of resolution. As the light sensitivity of the sensor is increased noise also increases. Digital ISO noise manifests itself in the form of off-colored pixels in an image, which is analogous to the grainy texture that is typically formed with high-speed film (Figure 2.6).

The highest usable ISO ranges of the camera can vary among camera manufacturers, and makes and models of cameras. It is recommended to determine what setting produces an "acceptable" level of noise, such that it does not diminish the evidentiary value of the photograph. The photographer should also be aware of any algorithms run by the camera that correct for ISO noise as these may use an interpolation process that could affect image resolution. An

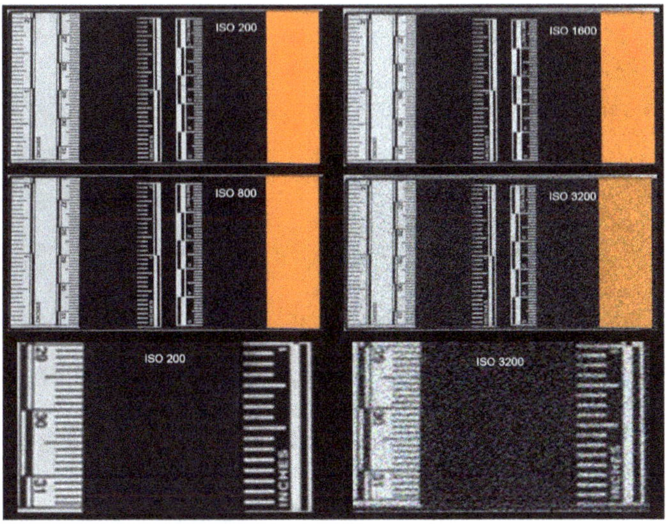

Figure 2.6 Increasing the ISO setting of a camera enhances the sensitivity of the sensor to light. However, as the sensitivity of the camera is increased "noise" develops resulting in grainy images. The subject was photographed using a DSLR camera with a macro lens. As the ISO was increased from 200 to 3200 chroma, noise developed in the images. The degree of noise observed at the upper ISO limit of a camera can vary across the manufacture, makes, and models of cameras available. Testing of the camera is often required to determine which setting produces the minimum acceptable levels of noise.

example of this would be chroma noise correction algorithms. Long exposures can also result in noise that is generally in the form of hot pixels. Hot pixels form as a result of uneven electrical discharges on the photoactive region of a sensor. This can result in bright pixels that can vary in color.

2.5 RECOMMENDED PHOTOGRAPHIC EQUIPMENT

A typical camera kit that is exclusively used for forensic imaging techniques should include the following equipment:

- Full-spectrum converted professional grade DSLR camera (with the hot mirror removed)
- Multiple memory cards
- Quality wide-angle zoom lenses
- Macro lenses
- Tripod and appropriate camera ball-head attachment
- Shutter release cables
- Flash units and cables

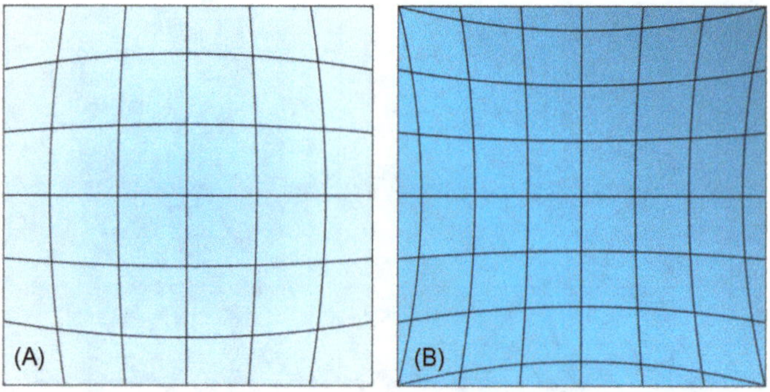

Figure 2.7 (A) An example of barrel distortion that can occur when a wide-angle zoom lens is set to full wide angle. (B) Pincushion distortion can occur when a wide-angle zoom lens is set to a fully zoomed position. The degree of distortion exhibited by a lens can vary with the make, model, and quality of the lens.

- UV transmission filters
- IR transmission filters
- Color barrier filters
- Hot mirror filter
- Inch and/or millimeter measurement scales, such as an ABFO No. 2 scale
- Extra batteries.

The selection of a professional grade DSLR camera is recommended because these cameras offer the most flexibility in terms of camera options in addition to manual control over these options. For example, a typical professional grade camera may allow you to select the bit depth of a TIFF or RAW file while a consumer grade camera, which can also be a DSLR, may not have these options available. In general, the fewer the options available on the camera, the more will be the limitations the photographer will experience when photographing evidence.

Wide-angle/zoom lenses can be very useful for the overall documentation of physical evidence. In a forensic imaging setting, a good quality wide-angle zoom lens can allow the photographer to zoom into an area of interest or zoom out to capture an establishing photograph without having to move the tripod setup. However, wide-angle zoom lenses may have inherent optical defects that can result in distortion of the photograph. Distortions that can be seen in these lenses can be of the chromatic or spherical type. A wide-angle zoom lens set to fully wide angle, for example, may exhibit barrel distortion at the edges of the photograph. Conversely, a wide-angle lens set to full zoom may exhibit pincushion distortion (Figure 2.7)

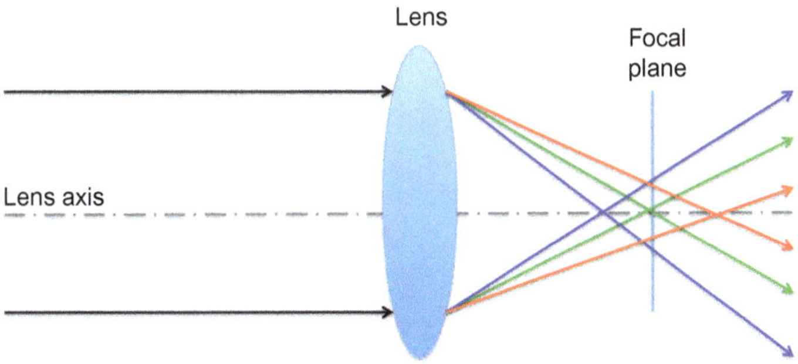

Figure 2.8 The image depicts refraction at the edges of a lens element, which can result in purple, red, or green fringing in areas of high contrast in a photo. This form of distortion is referred to as a chromatic aberration.

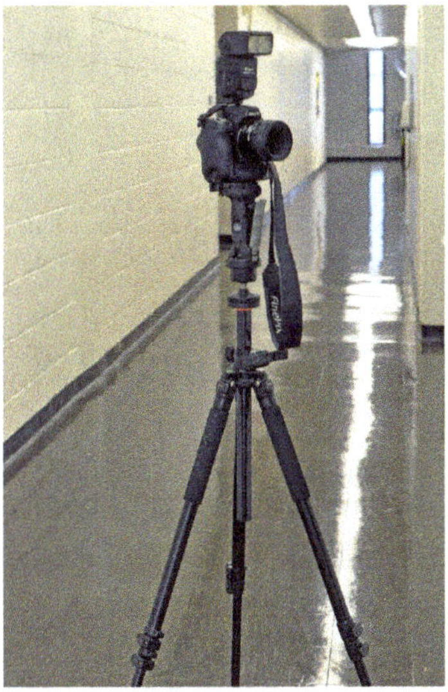

Figure 2.9 A DSLR camera normally mounted on a tripod. Tripods are necessary equipment when imaging with UV and narrowband light wavelengths. These imaging techniques require ambient light free environments to observe fluorescence. The imaging techniques for capturing fluorescence require long exposures. Tripods and shutter release cables are needed to minimize motion blur.

whereby the center of the photograph is distorted. Depending on the manufacture of the lens elements, refraction may occur as light passes through the lens. This form of aberration is referred to as chromatic and can manifest as a red, green, or purple tinge on areas of high contrast in an image (Figure 2.8). Although these forms of distortion are common in wide-angle zoom lenses, the degree of

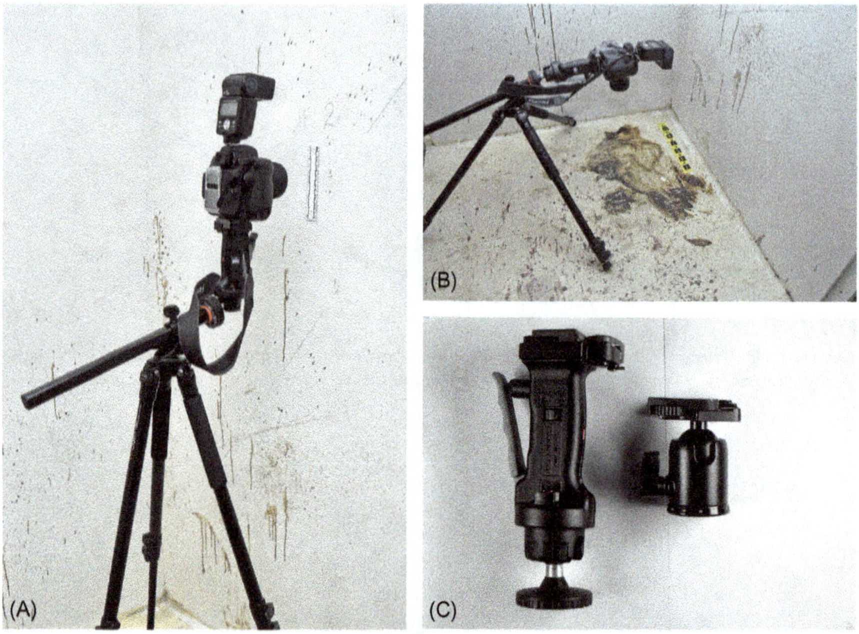

Figure 2.10 When selecting a tripod for use in forensic imaging, maximum flexibility should be considered so that various photographic scenarios can be accommodated. Tripods with articulating arms can facilitate the positioning of a camera in many different configurations. In image (A), a DSLR camera is mounted on the tripod that is configured for a close-up photograph of bloodstains on a wall. In image (B), the same camera–tripod setup is configured to photograph contact bloodstains on a floor. Image (C) depicts examples of ball-head mounts for a tripod. The ball-head can be used to further adjust the position of the camera relative to the subject.

distortion may vary with manufacturer and quality of the lens. If critical evidence is photographed with lenses that are prone to distortion, it may not be possible to obtain valuable information such as accurate measurements from a photograph. For this reason, macro lenses, which tend to exhibit less spherical aberrations, are recommended for any critical work. A macro lens is also an essential component of an ALS imaging kit.

Tripods and shutter release cables are necessary for ALS work, particularly in the crime scene or morgue setting. With the exception of IR imaging, most ALS imaging scenarios will require complete darkness in order to minimize ambient light contamination in a photograph. This means that exposure times will be generally be longer than 1/60 second and may be subject to motion blur if the camera or subject is moved. Tripods and shutter release cables aid in minimizing the motion of the camera. When selecting a tripod, the photographer should select one

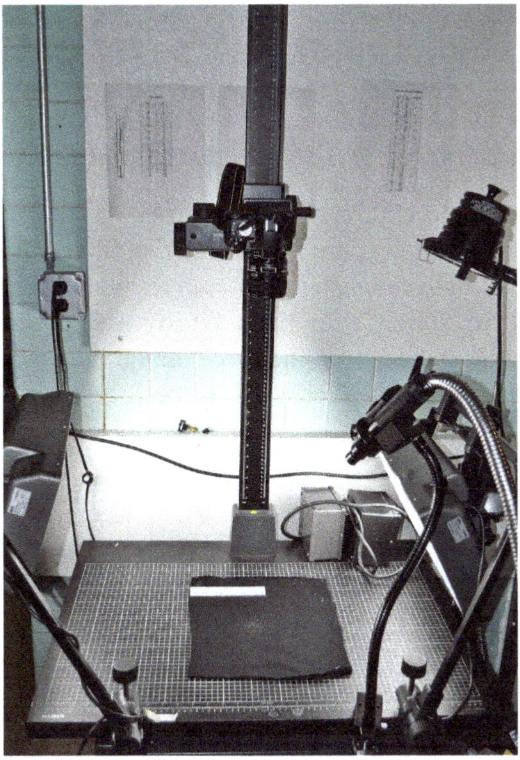

Figure 2.11 The image depicts a copy stand setup for forensic imaging. The camera is mounted on a column and can be raised or lowered as needed. The sides of the stand are also equipped with daylight corrected fluorescent lights that can be positioned as needed to provide even illumination of the subject. The light guide of an ALS is also depicted in addition to an incandescent flood lamp, which can be used to illuminate a subject for IR photography.

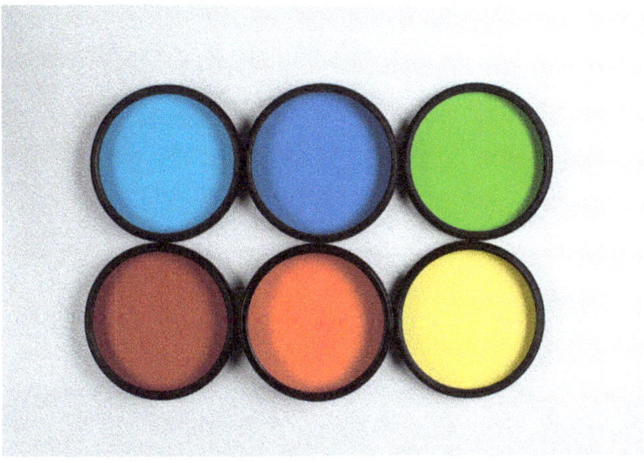

Figure 2.12 Color barrier filters can vary in color and density. These filters can be used to block light from an ALS to allow the visualization of fluorescence or to establish contrast using monochromatic settings. An ample selection of filters should be available to the forensic photographer to accommodate various imaging scenarios.

that he/she feels comfortable working with such that most shooting scenarios can be accommodated (Figures 2.9c and 2.10A–C). Fully adjustable tripods with articulating arms, coupled with a ball-head attachment, are recommended. In the laboratory setting, a fully adjustable copy stand is an indispensible piece of equipment (Figure 2.11).

In addition to the equipment, wide arrays of filters are needed to suit a variety of photographic needs. Barrier filters (Figure 2.12) can be used to block light from the light source, while visible light blocking filters that transmit UV or IR radiation are required for imaging in the non-visible portions of the electromagnetic spectrum. Specific filters and their use will be discussed in the following chapters.

CHAPTER 3

UV and Narrowband Visible Light Imaging

A forensic light source (FLS) is commonly used in the forensic setting to visualize evidence that may be difficult to detect with the naked eye. Fluorescence, phosphorescence, absorption, and reflection may all occur when evidence is illuminated with a light source creating contrast, thereby facilitating the recognition of evidentiary material. Many of the techniques used for ultraviolet (UV) and alternate light source (ALS) photography are similar and will be discussed in the same fashion. Documenting these findings, although challenging in the past where film cameras were used, is simplified with digital camera equipment. However, thorough knowledge of the camera equipment is essential. Because photography is being performed using narrow bands of light, the automatic focusing capabilities of the camera are not often usable. Documenting evidence under wavelength specific radiation often requires manual focusing with careful consideration for depth of field in the image. Additionally, working with narrow wavelengths of light means that exposure times will be much longer than usual. The use of a tripod or copy stand is often required under these conditions.

3.1 UV REFLECTANCE AND FLUORESCENCE PHOTOGRAPHY

Reflected UV photography captures an image where the radiation has been absorbed or reflected from the sample. This differs from UV fluorescence. With fluorescence, UV radiation is absorbed by the sample and the energy is reemitted at a longer wavelength, often in the visible portion of the spectrum. The disparity between wavelength absorbed and reemitted is referred to as *Stokes shift.* A filter is used to block the UV radiation from the source, allowing only the fluorescence to reach the camera sensor (Figure 3.1).

Reflected UV photography requires a filter that only allows UV radiation to reach the sensor and act as a barrier to all other wavelengths. The setup is illustrated in Figure 3.2. Alternatively, no filter can be used if the photography is conducted in a light-tight darkroom and the source only emits UV radiation, provided the subject does not

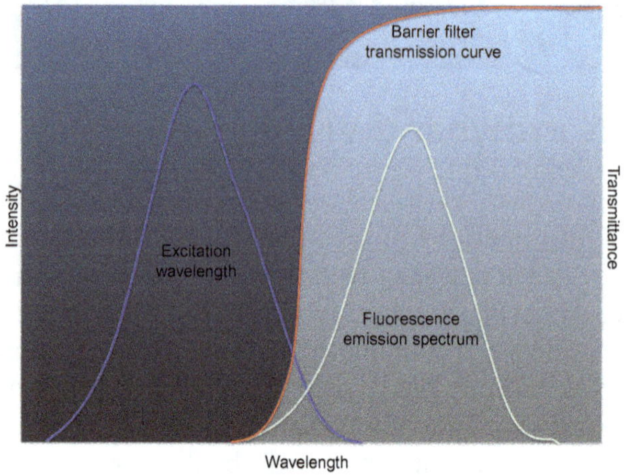

Figure 3.1 As mentioned in Chapter 1, fluorescence is the light emitted from a substance that has absorbed light. The wavelength of fluorescent light is longer than the excitation wavelength. The function of a barrier filter as illustrated is to block out light that is emitted by the light source so that the fluorescence can be observed. Here, the filter curve is representative of a longpass filter where light to the left of the filter is blocked and fluorescence occurs in the region where light is transmitted by the filter.

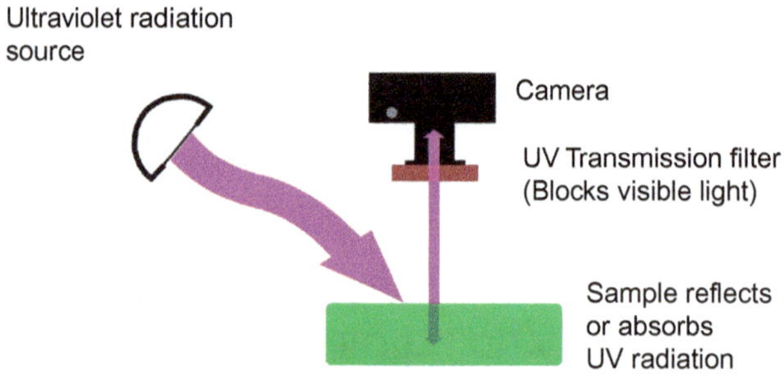

Figure 3.2 A basic setup for reflected UV imaging.

fluoresce. UV radiations are those wavelengths shorter than violet and therefore carry no color information. A digital, pure UV image should appear monochrome if a manual white balance is correctly performed. Subjects that reflect UV will appear bright, and subjects that absorb UV will appear dark.

The UV region ranges from approximately 10 to 400 nm. Below approximately 200 nm has been referred to as the vacuum UV region. At these frequencies, the radiation is strongly absorbed by the atmosphere, and studies would have to be carried out in a vacuum environment. For discussion purposes, we need to define the region of UV that silicon-based DSLR camera sensors are sensitive to. The UV region can be broken down into various subgroups and is largely industry dependent. For our purposes, the near-UV region is between approximately 300 and 400 nm (nearest to violet) and the far-UV region is between approximately 200 and 300 nm (furthest from violet).

UV photography can be used to enhance evidence such as

- Biological fluids
- Fingerprints
- Bruising
- Gunshot residues
- Fibers
- Documents.

3.2 PHOTOGRAPHIC EQUIPMENT

Cameras that have been modified or converted to full spectrum cameras, where the internal hot mirror has been removed, are only sensitive down to about 300 nm. Below 300 nm the sensitivity begins to decrease sharply. There is only a narrowband of UV radiation (between 300 and 400 nm) that can be recorded with a DLSR camera. If a modified camera is not feasible, there are several off-the-shelf cameras such as the Nikon DSLR D70, the D70s, and the D40 that are reported to be particularly suitable for UV photography. These cameras are known to have a hot mirror that transmits a suitable amount of UV radiation.

3.2.1 Lenses

Lens choice is often misunderstood when dealing with UV. Many people have been taught that silica glass and the coatings used on glass absorb UV, which is true. Modern lenses used for digital photography have coatings to block UV and contain multiple lens elements that also absorb UV. However, the glass and the coatings do not become effective until you approach 350 nm. So, your normal lenses could be used for reflected, near-UV photography. This will narrow the useful bandwidth of UV to about 350–400 nm. Films used for UV photography, such as the Kodak T-Max series, are sensitive into the far-UV region. In order to photograph the far-UV region using film, a different type of camera lens needed to be employed. Lenses such as the Nikon Nikkor 105 mm UV lens are typically made of quartz or fused silica and transmit well into the far-UV region. These lenses were expensive and are not readily available anymore, and probably got packed away with the 35-mm film equipment. There are some companies that have revisited the digital-UV application for astronomy purposes and produced lenses that transmit UV efficiently. Available on the market are the Jenoptik Coastal Optics *UV-VIS 105 mm APO* and *UV-VIS-IR 60 mm Apo Macro* lenses, but be prepared for the cost, and they are only fitted for Nikon F-mount cameras. The advantage of these lenses is that they are apochromatically corrected so the focus shift is eliminated.

There is also a focus shift associated with UV imaging. UV is shorter in wavelength than visible light and therefore gets refracted at a greater angle (Figure 3.3). This means that the UV radiation will come into focus in front of the image sensor. There are several ways to deal with the focus shift: (i) employ a DSLR that has a live view, (ii) buy an expensive apochromatic lens, or (iii) calibrate the lens.

3.2.2 Filters

The most familiar UV bandpass filter for reflected UV photography is the #18A as designated by Kodak. The transmission spectrum of the #18A is shown in Figure 3.4. The transmission specifications for other common UV bandpass filters are given in Table 3.1. By examining the transmission curve for the #18A, we notice that the filter transmits very efficiently between 250 and 400 nm with its peak at about 325 nm. The filter blocks visible radiation between 400 and 680 nm. There is a second bandpass area in the near-infrared (near-IR) region

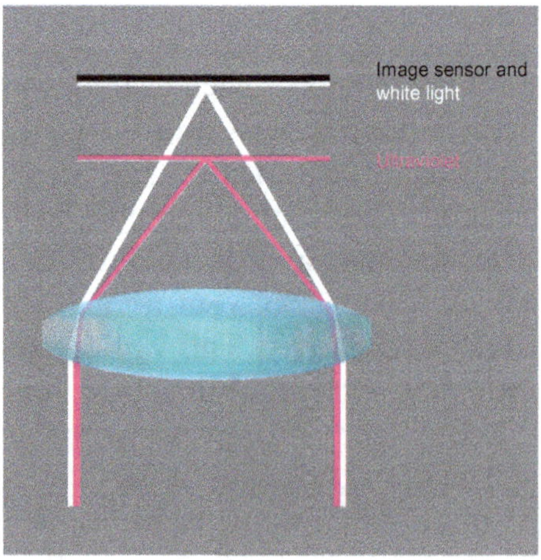

Figure 3.3 UV focus shift through a simple lens.

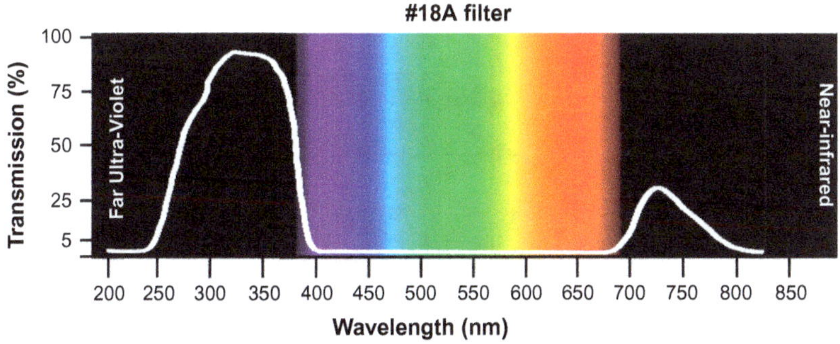

Figure 3.4 Transmission curve for the #18A filter.

between 680 and 800 nm. This unwanted transmission in the near-IR region is commonly called an IR leak. When using this filter, one must take special precautions to carefully control the illumination. For example, a tungsten light source emits near-UV, visible, and IR radiation. The majority of the energy is emitted in the IR. The #18A filter blocks the visible radiation. The digital camera, converted or not, will have a stronger spectral response in the IR compared to the UV. So, any image captured under these conditions will be dominated by the IR. In order to capture reflected UV radiation using a filter such as the #18A, the photography has to be conducted using a radiation source and in an environment that is free of IR radiation. There is a very good article authored by Richards (http://www.company7.com/library/nikon/Reflected_UV_Imaging_for_Forensics_V2.pdf) regarding reflected UV photography. He recommends the *Baader Venus* UV transmission filter. This filter has a UV bandpass from 325 to 390 nm. It also has a near-IR bandpass at 1150 nm, but this is beyond the sensitivity of a silicon-based digital camera sensor.

3.3 UV LIGHT SOURCES

Sources used for UV photography can be of two types: continuous and line. Continuous sources emit radiation where the intensity slowly changes as a function of wavelength. Line sources only emit a number of lines or wavelength bands over a limited wavelength range. Some common UV radiation sources are listed in Figure 3.5.

The black light fluorescent tubes that most of us have encountered at some point emit a band of radiation in the near-UV region around

Table 3.1 Approximate Bandpass Regions for Common UV Transmission Filters

	Kodak #18A	**Wood's Glass**	**Hoya U-340**	**Hoya U-350**	**Baader Venus UV**	**Schott UG-1**	**B + W 403**	**MidOpt BP324**
UV bandpass	310–400 nm	230–420 nm	260–390 nm	310–390 nm	320–380 nm	290–410 nm	290–400 nm	250–390 nm
IR bandpass	670–830 nm	670–1000 nm	680–750 nm, <5% T	690–800 nm <1% T	>1150 nm	690–1100 nm	700–1000 nm	680–820 nm

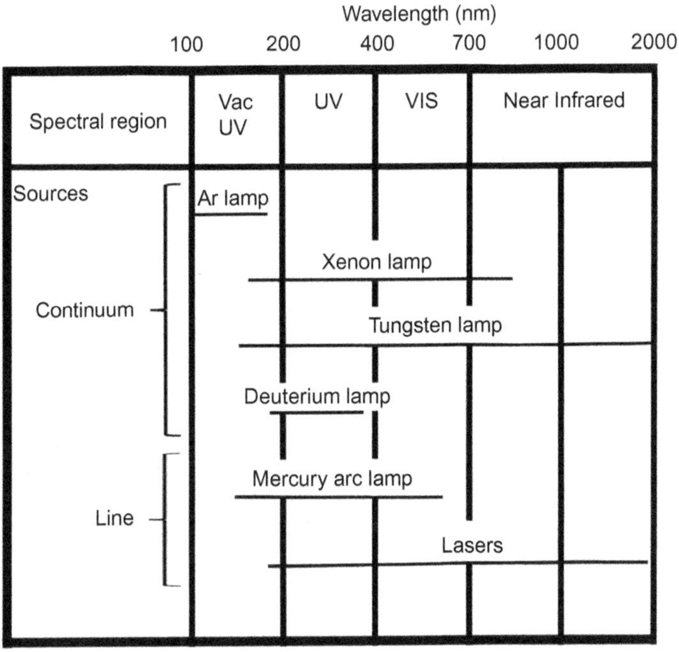

Figure 3.5 Sources that emit radiation in the UV spectral region.

365 nm along with some violet light. They also emit IR radiation typically near the end of the tube close to the contact points (Figure 3.6). In addition to the IR emission, these types of sources are not very intense and require longer exposure times. In order to photograph with only pure UV radiation, the source must be filtered.

For the forensic practitioner, the ALS provides the most convenient means of employing a spectrally pure UV source. Many of the common light source brands use a xenon arc source and a light guide. The LED flashlights can also be configured for pure UV photography. An issue with the LED models is that they are not as intense as the xenon arc sources and tend to produce hotspots due to uneven illumination (Figure 3.7). Reflected UV and ALS photography will also require longer exposure times (seconds). One way to deal with hotspots and weak sources is to use a technique called "painting with light." This technique is used in low light conditions. The camera shutter is set to a long exposure and then opened. The light source is then moved back and forth systematically over the subject for the duration of the shutter in an effort to illuminate the subject evenly.

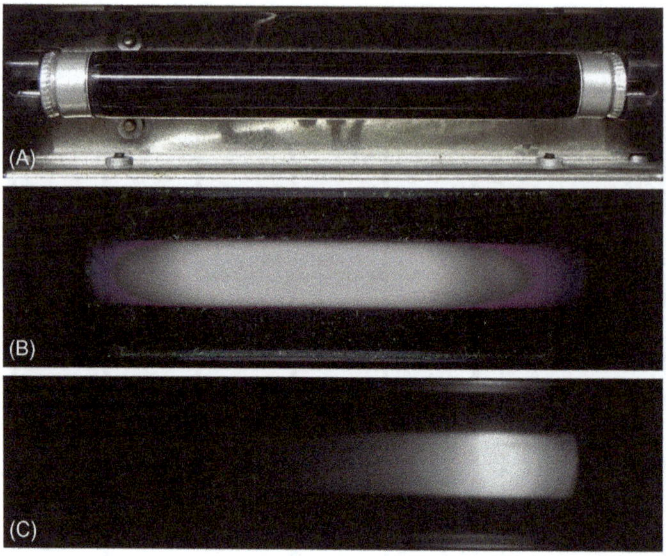

Figure 3.6 (A) UV lamp in the off position. (B) The lamp turned on, photographed in a darkroom with the lights off and no filter over the lens. (C) Illustrates the IR leak. Image photographed in a darkroom with a Kodak Wratten #87 placed over the camera lens.

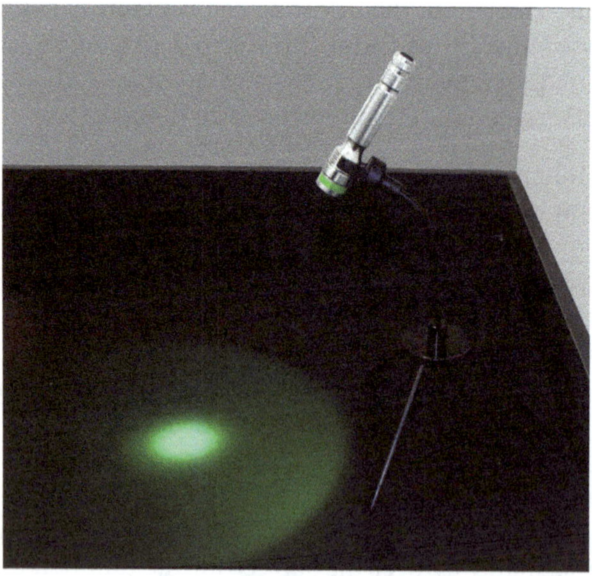

Figure 3.7 Illustrates the hotspot and uneven illumination that can be produced by an LED flashlight unit.

Electronic flash units with a xenon source also have a UV output, but only if the straw-colored yellow filter that can be seen around the bulb is absent. This filter absorbs the UV output from the flash head. There are flash units that were designed for UV photography. The Nikon SB-140 UV-IR flash was designed for the F-series and N-series cameras (film). This system was designed for use with one of three filters fitted over the flash: the SW-5V filter between 400 and 1000 nm for visible light, the SW-5 IR filter between 750 and 1000 nm for IR radiation, and the SW-5 UV filter between 300 and 400 nm for UV radiation. The UV filter also has the resolute IR leak at wavelengths longer than 650 nm.

Whenever possible, the evidence should be taken to the laboratory where it can be photographed under controlled conditions. To summarize, reflected UV photography requires several considerations:

- A filter over the lens is required that transmits UV radiation and acts as a barrier to visible light, not only from the ambient environment but also any fluorescence that could be induced from illuminating the evidence with UV radiation.
- If the UV transmission filter has an IR leak, then a filtered source is required that only emits a band of UV radiation.
- If the UV transmission filter is an efficient barrier to visible light and IR radiation (i.e., Baader filter), then any source that has an UV output could be used.

3.4 EFFECTS OF UV RADIATION

UV radiation is higher in energy than visible light; one of the properties of UV radiation is that it can be used to induce fluorescence in many substances that have a system of conjugated bonds. After a portion of a molecule is promoted to an electronically excited state by the absorption of electromagnetic radiation, several things can happen; one of the most apparent is fluorescence. The species can reemit the absorbed radiation and fall into a lower excited state or the ground state. This emission of radiation is referred to as fluorescence. The fluorescence emission is usually longer in wavelength than the absorption radiation.

One of the drawbacks in working with UV radiation is its high energy. The induced fluorescence by the absorption of UV radiation breaks chemical bonds. The intensity of the fluorescence emission can

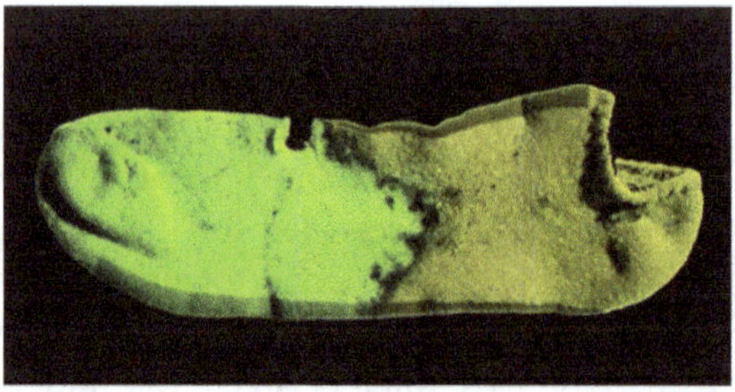

Figure 3.8 Difference in fluorescent activity of a sock that had been partially buried for a period of at least 2 weeks. Photographed using a tunable light source, 415 nm excitation, and yellow barrier filter.

decay if the subject is exposed to UV radiation for an extended period of time. Figure 3.8 depicts an athletics sock that was partially buried outdoors for a period of at least two weeks. The left side of the image depicts the buried portion of the sock and is still fluorescently active. The right side was exposed to UV radiation of the sun and exhibits no fluorescent activity.

3.5 ALTERNATE LIGHT SOURCES

The terms ALS, FLS, and high-intensity tunable wavelength light source are often used interchangeably. They all have several things in common: (i) an intense source that emits radiation over the UV, visible, and IR spectral regions and (ii) a series of specially designed filters that allow the user to select narrow bands of radiation, typically in the 20–100 nm range.

Not all light sources are created equal, and several factors need to be considered before purchasing a light source:

- Intensity of the source
- Number of bands or wavelength colors to select from
- Portability/user friendliness.

When using tunable wavelength light sources, it is important to understand which barrier filters correspond to the wavelength of light being used. Barrier filters serve to block light that is transmitted from the instrument and create contrast necessary to visualize and photograph evidence. It is important to realize that manufacture supplied goggles do not necessarily correspond to photographic filters of the same or similar color. The proper photographic barrier filter must also

Table 3.2 Relative Guide for Wavelength and Barrier Filter Combinations

Wavelength	Barrier Filter
300–400 nm (UV)	UV reflectance/UV transmitting (VIS blocking)
300–400 nm (UV)	UV fluorescence: clear (UV absorbing) or yellow
410–450 nm	Yellow
455–520 nm	Orange
530–700 nm	Red
700–1100 nm (IR)	IR transmitting (UV/VIS blocking)

be selected so as to prevent light contamination from the instrument that may reduce the contrast between fluorescence emission and its background in the photograph.

3.6 WAVELENGTH AND BARRIER FILTER SELECTION

The barrier filter selected when examining physical evidence is contingent on the wavelength of light selected from the light source. The ultimate goal of the barrier filter is to block out the radiation from the source that is reflected from the physical evidence. Table 3.2 should help in selecting the appropriate barrier filter when using a selectable wavelength source.

Photographic filters may not block light to the same extent as the barrier filter or goggles to cover the eyes that are supplied from the manufacturer. For this reason, it is important that the examiner visualizes the evidence through both the barrier filter and the camera filter. The use of a filter over the camera lens that is not efficient at blocking the radiation from the light source may mask the intensity of the fluorescence emission. If proper filter is not utilized, there is the possibility that the fluorescence may not be detected (Figure 3.9A and B and see photographic examples of light leakage through a filter can be seen in Figures 3.14C and D). A simple way to determine if a photographic filter adequately blocks light from an ALS is to simply put the filter in front of the light guide. If light is transmitted, then a different filter needs to be selected.

Understanding and selecting the appropriate filter are the most important part of ALS photography. The following list of terms describes nomenclature that a photographer should be familiar with:

Absorption: Attenuation of electromagnetic radiation lost through transformation to another form of energy, such as heat, while passing through a material.

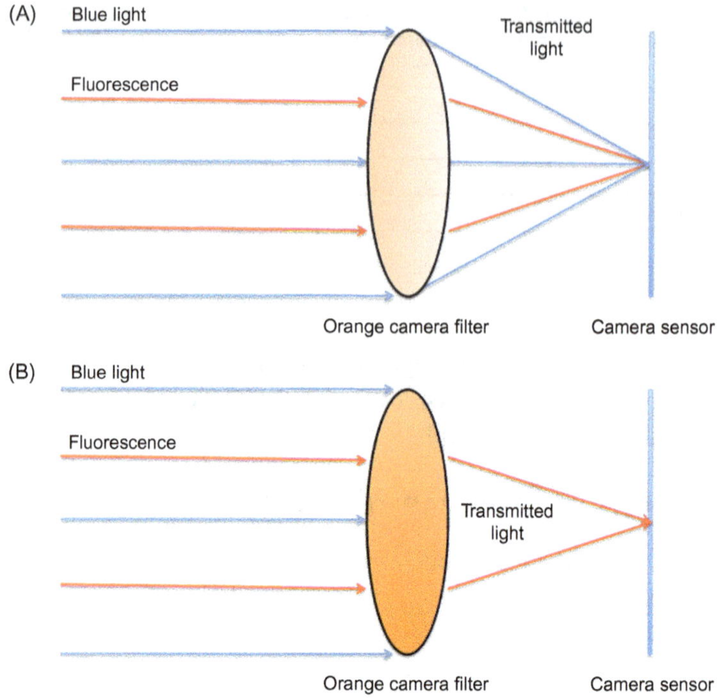

Figure 3.9 (A) When evidence is illuminated with a light source, the evidence may reflect and absorb radiation in addition to fluorescence. The function of a barrier filter is to block out light that is reflected back toward the camera so that fluorescence can be seen. This is a graphical representation of a filter over a camera lens that allows light reflected from the evidence to pass into the camera. This may mask the intensity of the fluorescence and any weak fluorescence might not be detected. (B) When a proper barrier filter is used, excitation illumination from an ALS should be blocked. The induced photoluminescence passes through the filter to the camera sensor and the resulting photograph will depict a better representation of the fluorescing material or stains.

Bandwidth: A wavelength range used to denote a specific part of the spectrum that passes electromagnetic radiation through a filter.

Bandpass filter: Filter designed to transmit radiation only within a selected band of wavelengths. These filters can be classified as narrow or wide bandpass filters, depending on the required bandwidth.

Barrier filters: Filters that are designed to suppress or block the excitation wavelengths and allow only selected fluorescent emission wavelengths to pass toward the detector.

Cut-off filter: The wavelength where there is a transition from a region of high transmission to a region of low transmission. This cut-off wavelength commonly refers to the 5% absolute transmission.

Cut-on filter: The area where there is a transition from a region of low transmission to an adjacent spectral region of high transmission. The term is often used to specify the wavelength location of a longpass filter. The wavelength of the 5% absolute transmission is commonly used as the cut-on wavelength.
Filter: An optical element that transmits selected wavelengths of radiation while blocking or absorbing all other wavelengths of radiation.
Hot mirror: A type of filter that contains a dielectric coating designed to reflect the IR region of the spectrum and transmit the visible region. It is used for applications where near-IR radiation needs to be removed from the light source.
Interference filter: A type of filter made up of several metallic and dielectric layers of material. An interference filter produces high spectral transmittance over a very narrow band of wavelengths.
Longpass filter: A type of filter where the transmission band is longer in wavelength than the region blocked. For example, longpass filter blocks visible radiation (400–700 nm) and transmits near-IR radiation (700–1200 nm).
Optical density: Describes the amount of energy that can pass through an optical element. It is directly related to the transmittance of the material, which is the ability of light to propagate through a given medium.
Shortpass filter: A type of filter where the transmission band is shorter in wavelength than the region blocked.
Transmission: Transmittance refers to the percentage of radiation that can pass through an optical element.
Wood's glass: An optical filter coated with nickel oxide that was invented by the physicist Robert Wood (1919) at the turn of the twentieth century. The filter blocks most visible light with the exception of violet and transmits both UV and IR radiation. Wood's glass was commonly used to form the envelope around UV fluorescent tubes (black lights).
Wratten filter: A type of filter created by dissolving organic dyes in a gelatin material to achieve the desired spectral performance. The gelatin liquid and dye combination is then coated onto a supportive substrate until it has dried. After removal from the substrate, the film is coated with lacquer for protection. Although the filters are coated, they should be handled only by the edges or in the corners to avoid damage.

3.7 APPLICATIONS OF UV REFLECTANCE AND FLUORESCENCE PHOTOGRAPHY

3.7.1 Fibers and Trace Evidence

Fluorescence can be used as a tool to further aid the characterization of both colored and colorless fibers. For example, a tunable light source can be used to search for "target fibers" that possess fluorescence characteristics (Figure 3.10). Fiber fluorescence can be attributed to a number of factors. Animal fibers such as wool and many commercial polymers exhibit their own characteristic fluorescence. The incorporation of colored dyestuffs that have the ability to fluoresce and the exposure to the fluorescent whitening agents found in household laundry detergents also contribute to the fluorescence of a fiber.

Due to the presence of certain colored impurities, textile fibers do not appear absolutely white. Many organic materials do not look completely white; they tend to absorb more blue-violet radiation, and in consequence appear to have a yellowish hue in reflected light. Even after treatment by chemical bleaching, fibers still possess a slight

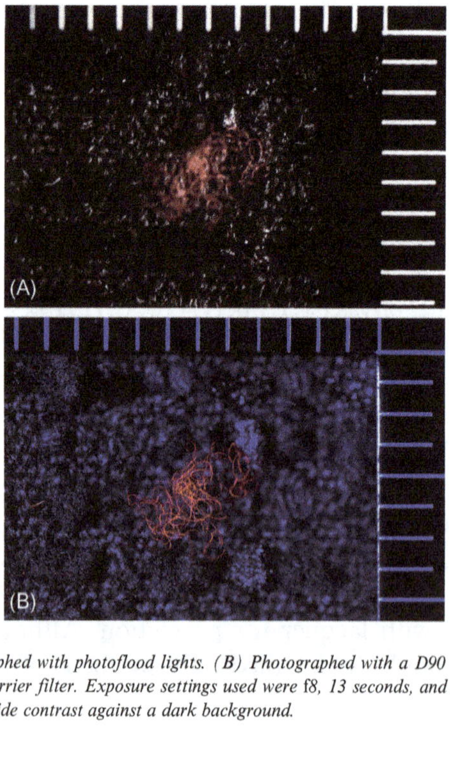

Figure 3.10 (A) Photographed with photoflood lights. (B) Photographed with a D90 Camera using 455 nm illumination and an orange barrier filter. Exposure settings used were f8, 13 seconds, and ISO 200. The fluorescence properties of the fiber provide contrast against a dark background.

yellow appearance. Fluorescent whitening agents counteract the yellowish appearance of fabrics by absorbing short wavelength light in the near-UV region of the spectrum and reemit part of that light in the blue region of the visible spectrum that the human eye perceives as a "brilliant white."

Figure 3.11A shows a photomicrograph of an unwashed fluorescent orange nylon fiber in cross section. Figure 3.11B shows a different orange fiber, from the same source, in cross section that has been washed with a household laundry detergent that contained an optical brightener. It can be seen that the addition of the optical brightener appears as a surface characteristic and does not penetrate significantly into the fiber structure as evident by the *blue halo* around the perimeter of the fiber. It does, however, significantly change the perceived fluorescence of the fiber. The cross sections of both fibers were photographed using a Leitz Ortholux II microscope equipped with a Leitz Ploemopak Fluorescence Illuminator and A2 filter cube. Cube A2 has an excitation range of 360–370 nm, with fluorescence emissions being detectable above 400 nm.

Certain minerals display fluorescence characteristics (Figure 3.12). However, fluorescence is not always a reliable method for mineral identification. Certain minerals of the same species from different geographic locations may fluoresce differently. Once a mineral has been identified through microscopic or instrumental analysis, its fluorescence properties can sometimes be used to identify geographic origin.

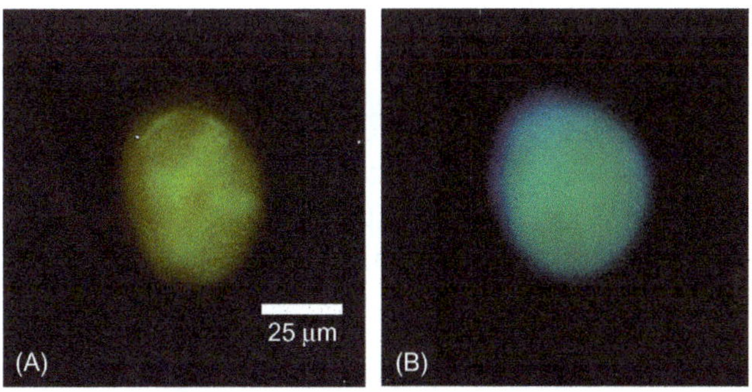

Figure 3.11 Cross-sectional view of fluorescence in an unwashed orange nylon fiber (A), and the fluorescence of another orange fiber (B) from the same source washed in laundry detergent. Magnification 200×.

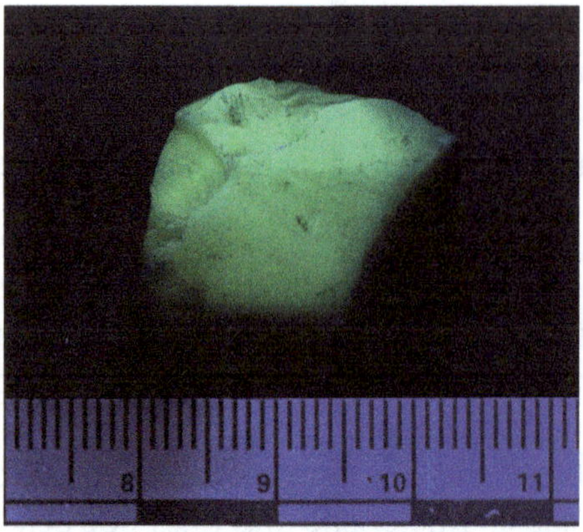

Figure 3.12 Native fluorescence of Opal mined from Humboldt Co., Nevada. Photographed with a Nikon D90 camera with exposure settings f16, 30 seconds, ISO 200, 365 nm excitation radiation, and no filter over the camera lens.

Skeletal remains can fluoresce under UV radiation and blue-violet light, especially when the soft tissue has decomposed and bones have entered a dry state or have been bleached white by the sun. If soft tissue, soil, or debris covers the skeletal remains, the fluorescence emission of the osseous material can be masked.

Barrier filters can help to suppress the background and increase contrast between the bones and the debris found in soil as well as minerals found in soil that may also fluoresce. A yellow barrier filter can be used for UV radiation or blue-violet light and will help create greater contrast between bones fragments and the background (Figure 3.13).

3.7.2 Gunshot Residue

When a firearm is discharged, the projectile along with burnt and partially burnt gunpowder, as well as gases produced by the combustion of the gunpowder and primer, are expelled from the barrel. At a close range, these residues can be deposited onto a victim or nearby objects. These residues can form a pattern that can be useful in estimating the muzzle-to-target distance or how far away the gun was from the target when it was discharged.

Gunshot residues are expelled from the gun barrel at high velocities, on average at a rate of 400–800 fps. These particles have a small mass and decelerate quickly. As a general rule, gunshot residues

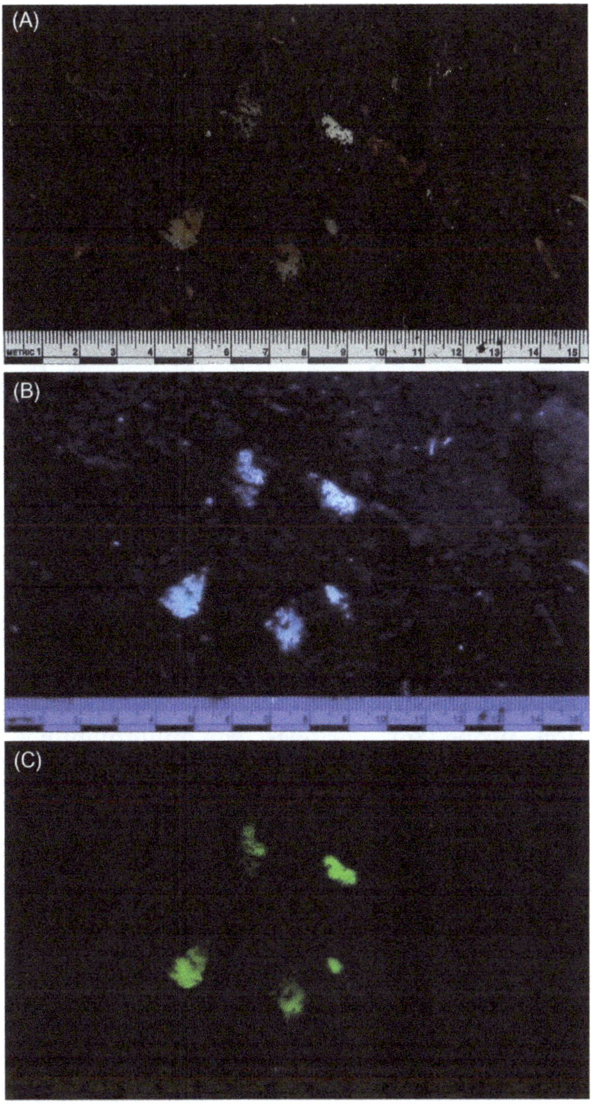

Figure 3.13 Bone fragments, nonhuman, recovered from a soil sample. (A) Recorded using normal flash photography. (B) Recorded using Nikon Coolpix P100 camera with exposure settings f6.3, 8 seconds, ISO 200, 365 nm excitation radiation, and no filter over the camera lens. (C) Also recorded with a Nikon Coolpix P100 camera with exposure settings f3.5, 8 seconds, ISO 200, 365 nm excitation radiation, and a yellow filter over the camera lens. Note how the yellow filter reduces the background fluorescence.

produced from handguns will not travel more than a couple of feet; however, residues produced from a long gun can travel further. At close range, these residues have enough energy to embed in skin or clothing.

Gunshot residue can be difficult to visualize if the residue is deposited onto dark colored clothing, the victim has dark pigmented skin, or the residue is concealed by blood. Gunshot residue is particularly labile and can be lost readily. A nondestructive approach is therefore necessary prior to chemical and instrumental analysis.

Fluorescence can be induced in the partially burnt organic constituents of gunshot residue. The best contrast is usually obtained by using blue light and an orange barrier filter (Figure 3.14A–D).

Pizzola (1998) studied the photoluminescence of gunshot residues extensively. The technique involves treating the gunshot residues *in situ* with 1M hydrogen chloride (1M HCl) followed by immersion in liquid nitrogen. The chloride ion can form a complex with the fine vaporous lead, antimony, and any such metal deposits that may reside on the particulate. At super-cold temperatures (liquid nitrogen), the metal chloride complex will photoluminesce using short wavelength radiation. In general, reducing the temperature of a substance increases its luminescence intensity. Using 254 nm short wavelength, UV excitation can induce luminescence from the vaporous lead portion of the residue. With 365 nm long wavelength, UV excitation propellant particles can photoluminesce and the vaporous lead is suppressed. This is a nondestructive technique to visualize both the vaporous lead and the particulate pattern residues from the same target without having to perform a transfer method (Figure 3.15).

3.7.3 Bruising, Bite Marks, and Ligature Marks

Bruise marks, ligature marks, bite marks, and any injury that results in damage to skin and/or small blood vessels beneath the skin can be illuminated with near-UV and visible radiation to establish contrast. There are a few basic ideas behind the ability to document physical injuries with a tunable light source. When bodily tissue is damaged, blood may be released into the interstitial spaces surrounding small vessels near the injury site, creating a bruise. During the healing process, melanin in the tissue may also accumulate in the areas of an injury resulting in hyperpigmentation around the injury site. As a result, tissues that are injured may absorb and reflect radiation differently than noninjured tissue. It is these differences in the

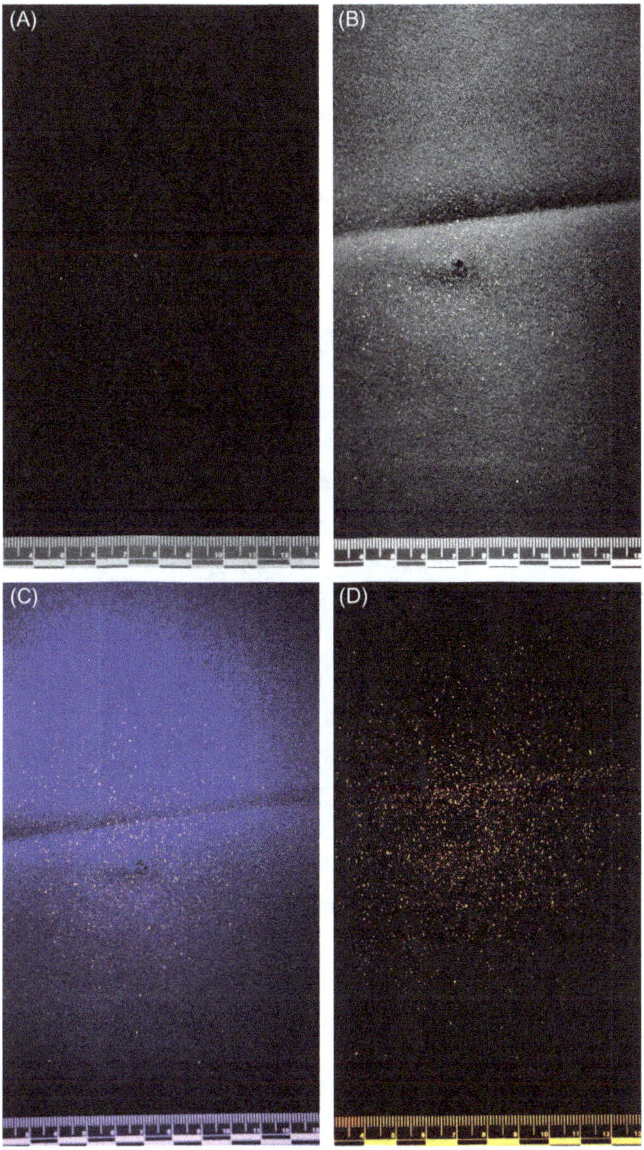

Figure 3.14 (A) Gunshot residue deposited on a black colored, 100%, cotton t-shirt. Image recorded with normal flash photography. (B) Gunshot residue photographed using white light from a high-intensity, tunable wavelength light source positioned at an oblique angle. (C) This photograph depicts the same GSR pattern from (A) and (B). In this photograph, the image was recorded using blue light with a bandwidth of 430–470 nm and a Tiffen orange 21 filter. The filter used for this image does not adequately block light from the ALS. While some native particle fluorescence is seen, the degree to which fluorescence emission is obscured by the light from the ALS can be noted when compared to the image of the same target in (D) that was taken with a deeper orange filter. The image was captured with a Nikon D300s camera using the following exposure settings: f8.0, 4 seconds, and ISO 200. (D) Native fluorescence of partially burned propellant. Image recorded using blue light with a bandwidth of 430–470 nm and a deep orange (YA2) filter. Image captured with a Nikon D300s camera using the following exposure settings: f8.0, 6 seconds, and ISO 200.

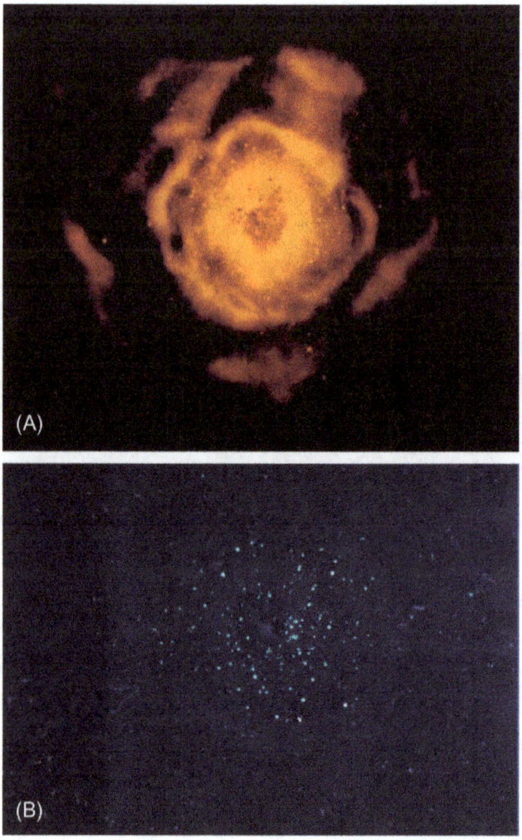

Figure 3.15 Short versus long wavelength excitation post treatment with 1M HCl and liquid nitrogen. (A) 254 nm excitation with an orange filter, the vaporous lead fluoresces brightly obscuring the particulate residue. (B) Photographed using 365 nm excitation (no filter) on the same pattern A; the particulate fluoresces with no interference from the lead. Images courtesy of Dr. Peter A. Pizzola.

response to light that we aim to capture when documenting injuries with the ALS.

Depending on the nature of the injury, certain wavelengths of light should be considered. While UV radiation (short wavelength) may provide enough excitation energy to induce fluorescence, it does not penetrate past the surface of the skin very well. UV can be used to document surface characteristics of the skin and superficial injuries such as scratches cuts, and bite marks. Radiation longer in wavelength than near-UV will have a better depth of penetration into tissue and should be used for imaging bruises and injuries that may be healing.

3.8 DOMESTIC VIOLENCE INJURIES

When examining domestic violence cases where the victim has survived, the circumstances of the case, the time, and the type of injury need to be carefully considered. A review of medical records or an interview with a physician who is familiar with the case should be performed prior to the examination. It is not unusual for these types of cases to go unreported for several days, if not weeks, after the incident. Attempts to image old injuries may require cycling through radiation bands from the near-UV region into the near-IR to determine the best wavelength for illumination and photo documentation of an injury. The location of the injury also needs to be considered. Injuries that occur deep into tissue may require illumination between the green and the red regions of the electromagnetic spectrum as these wavelengths can penetrate well into the dermal and subcutaneous regions of the skin. The amount of light reflected or absorbed by the subject's skin is subject to bioindividual variation. Factors such as the presence of skin diseases, skin color, melanin content, and/or skin pigment disorders may limit any observable contrast and challenge attempts at photographic documentation (Figure 3.16).

Figure 3.17A shows a photograph of the right leg, inner thigh region, of a domestic violence victim. Russian words were carved into her leg with a razor. In Figure 3.17B, 450 nm illumination from a SPEX HandScope and a yellow barrier filter was used to enhance the scarring in order to make the lettering more visible.

Figure 3.18A shows a photograph of a person who was bound at the wrists with rope. The top image here was captured shortly after the restraints were removed, and the bottom image is a photograph of the wrist using reflected UV illumination, in a darkroom, with a yellow filter 1 day after the restraints were removed. The images in Figure 3.18B were captured 2 days after the restraints were removed. As time progresses and the injury site begins to heal, the window of opportunity to document the injury diminishes. This is also dependent on the severity of the injury, location of the injury, and some people's natural tendency to bruise easier.

With domestic violence cases, the cooperation of the victim may be limited giving the photographer a small window of opportunity to document any injuries using these techniques. Therefore, there are several photographic and equipment considerations that have to be taken into

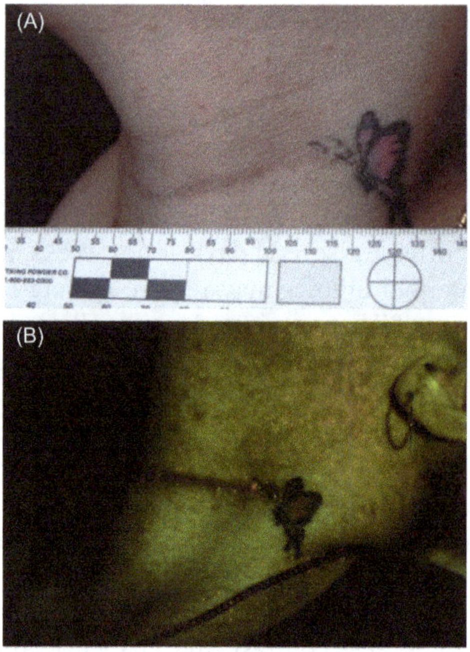

Figure 3.16 (A) Depicts a well-healed scar on the neck of a domestic violence victim whose throat was cut with a "cheese" knife. Ironically, the laceration was described as "superficial." (B) This image was recorded with 420 nm illumination and a yellow barrier filter. Contrast is greatly enhanced between the scar and the surrounding tissue. The orange colored fluorescent specs are the result of a common fungal skin infection.

account when imaging domestic violence cases. The photographic techniques used in this form of documentation need to be carried out in the absence of ambient light, which necessitates the use of long exposures and cameras that are capable of high ISO with minimal ISO noise or long exposure noise. Tripods, shutter release cables, and high quality lenses are necessary to minimize motion blur from the victim which can negatively impact images that are of evidentiary value. In addition to this equipment, a good set of filters are required that complement the various setting light sources being used. Thorough knowledge of the camera equipment and light sources is ultimately required to minimize the length of the documentation process and troubleshoot any imaging problems encountered.

3.8.1 Deceased Victims

An autopsy examining a deceased victim for bruise, bite, or ligature mark patterns requires a visual examination under white light for any

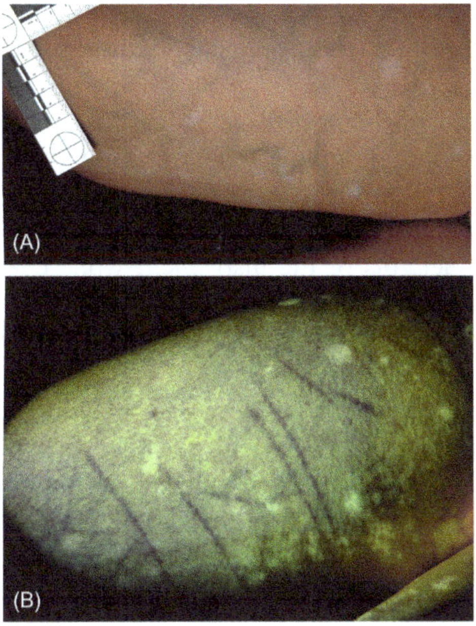

Figure 3.17 (A) Recorded using normal flash photography. (B) Recorded with a Nikon D3x camera with the following exposure settings: f4.0, 2.5 seconds, ISO 1600, 450 nm illumination, and a yellow barrier filter.

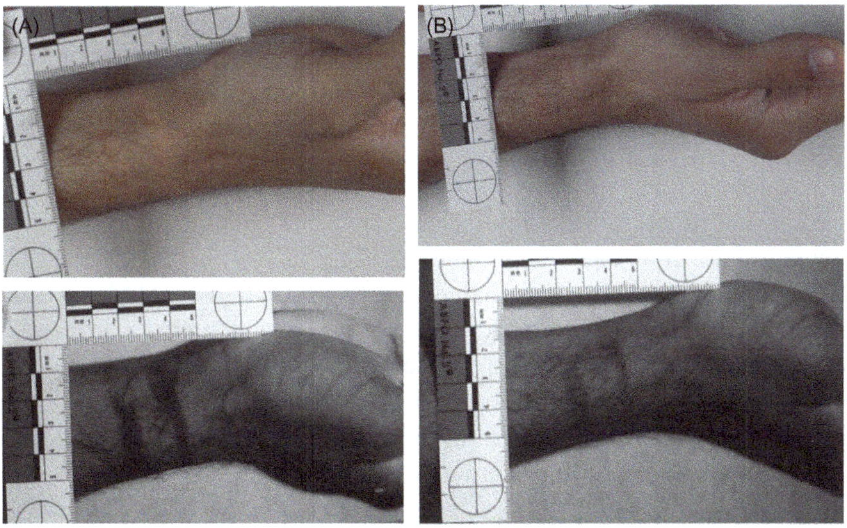

Figure 3.18 (A) Top image captured using normal flash photography shortly after the restraints were removed from the wrist. Bottom image recorded 1 day after the restraints were removed using a D200 camera, in a darkroom with 365 nm illumination and a yellow filter. Exposure settings were f10.0, 1.6 seconds, and ISO 500. (B) Top image captured 2 days after removal of the restraints using normal flash photography. Bottom image recorded 2 days after the restraints were removed using Nikon D200 camera, in a darkroom with 365 nm illumination and a yellow filter. Exposure settings were f10.0, 1.6 seconds, and ISO 500.

visible findings followed by careful examinations under various settings with an ALS. A good starting point is the use of the CSS setting on a SPEX instrument or a comparable broadband wavelength setting. Examination using a broadband pass setting may reveal not only bruising but also the presence of biological evidence in the form of fluorescent stains or fluorescent trace materials such as hairs, fibers, and/or particles that may be of investigative relevance. Cycling through the wavelengths of the instrument while changing barrier filters will also allow the examiner to determine the effects of the various wavelengths of light on the subject's skin, which may vary depending on the extent of decomposition. Keep in mind that the depth of penetration for each wavelength of light differs. While shortwave UV is highly energizing, it does not penetrate deep into tissue. UV wavelengths can be used to effectively image superficial injuries to the skin. As the wavelength setting on the light source is increased, light will penetrate deeper into tissue and this will generally allow imaging of injuries beneath the surface of the skin.

The basis of imaging injuries of forensic relevance rests on the notion that damaged tissue differs from nondamaged tissue. In the case of a bruise, the injury involves the rupture of blood vessels causing the release of blood into the interstitial spaces surrounding the injury site. Because of this, and several other factors, areas of damaged skin will absorb and reflect light differently than nondamaged skin. The goal of ALS imaging is to capture these differences in light absorption and reflection with a photograph.

The examiner additionally has to gauge the benefits of this form of imagery and that requires an understanding of the purpose of the photograph. Is the injury such that it can be compared to other physical evidence of the case and additionally, what would such a comparison require? Does the photographic technique enhance the injury and improve the chances of a comparison to an object that created the injury? These factors may dictate the equipment selected for photography and the photographic setup used.

As shown in Figure 3.19, the victim sustained blunt force (Figure 3.20) impacts to the face resulting in a patterned abrasion on the right cheek. The injury was imaged using a SPEX HandScope set to UV (310–390 nm), 415 nm, and CSS (blue-violet to green). While all produced some level of contrast, the 415 nm image reveals the most

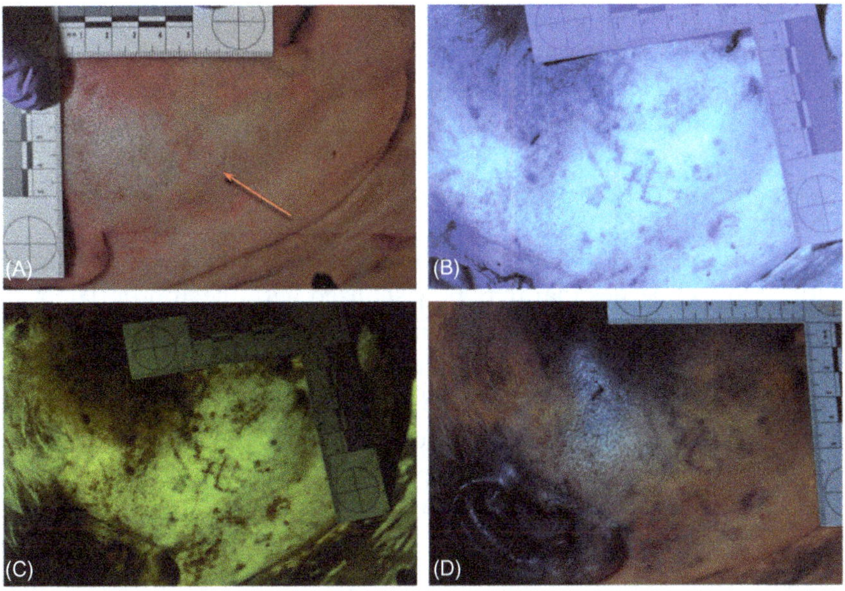

Figure 3.19 In these images, the victim sustained blunt force impacts to the face, which resulted in a patterned abrasion. The injury was imaged at various wavelengths with a Nikon D3x camera in aperture priority mode. Image (A) was taken with flash photography. In image (B), the injury was photographed with UV (310–390 nm) and no filter was used over the camera lens. In image (C), the injury was illuminated with 415 nm with a Tiffen yellow 12 filter. Image (D) was photographed using the CSS setting of a SPEX HandScope with a Tiffen orange 21 filter over the camera lens.

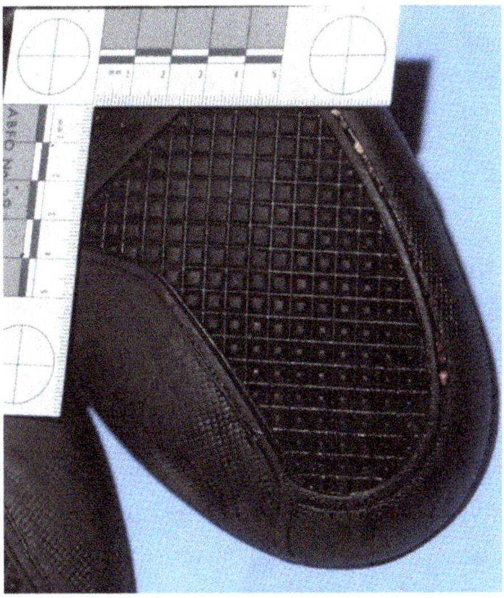

Figure 3.20 This image details the footwear pattern of the shoe believed to be responsible for the patterned abrasions imaged in Figure 3.19.

because of the depth of penetration inherent in the wavelength of light selected and peak absorption of blood in the 420 nm range. The image taken with the CSS setting shows a hotspot on the cheekbone area resulting from a filter leak (Figures 3.19 and 3.20).

3.8.2 Fingerprints

There are components of fingerprint residues that possess inherent fluorescent properties that may be visualized with the appropriate radiation source without any development. The radiation source needs to be intense and the work has been traditionally done with powerful, expensive lasers. The sources used in FLS units can be described as intense, but much of the energy is lost through filtration, and the intensity is not comparable to the output from a collimated laser source. Early research to induce native fluorescence from fingerprint residue was performed by Menzel (1999), a scientist at the Xerox Research Center of Canada. An argon-ion laser (green) was used to induce fluorescence (yellow) from the residue. One drawback is that the fluorophores present in fingerprint residue are in low concentration giving the laser technique varying degrees of success.

There are many types of fingerprint powders produced that fluoresce upon exposure to UV radiation, laser illumination, and various wave bands of light. These types of fingerprint powders are useful for the visualization of latent prints deposited on complex surfaces that would present a contrast problem if developed with traditional black or white powders. By selecting the correct colored powder, wavelength, and barrier filter, it is possible to minimize the colored background that would otherwise obscure the print.

Traditionally, there have been issues with fluorescent powders, and for a valid reason. Many of the fluorescent powders, when examined under magnification using a microscope, are much smaller in particle size compared to their black and white counterparts. Many of the fluorescent powders also contain pollen grains, or fillers, which are used to add bulk. With the smaller particle size, the powder tends to get deposited into the furrows of the fingerprint obscuring the detail of the print. A technique that has proven useful is to dust the item with an appropriate fluorescent powder, and then dust the item again with a feather brush that has been used with black powder. The second treatment

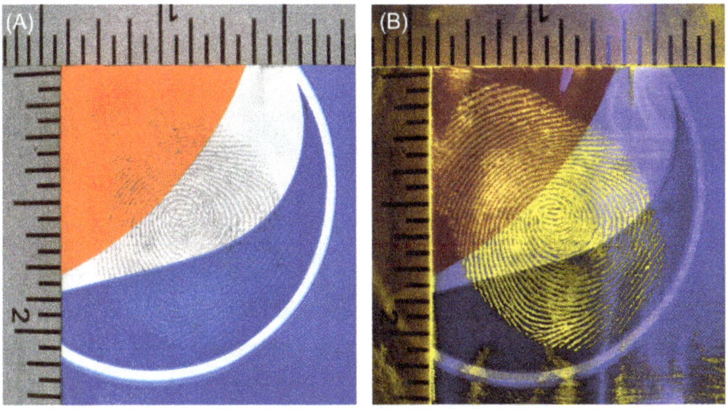

Figure 3.21 Fingerprint first developed with cyanoacrylate fuming and then dusting with a magnetic orange fluorescent powder. The excess fluorescent powder was removed by redusting the print with a feather brush and black powder. (A) Recorded with photoflood light illumination source. (B) Recorded with a Nikon D90 camera using 455 nm excitation and an orange barrier filter. The exposure settings were f16.0, 15 seconds, and ISO 200.

with the black powder removes much of the excess fluorescent powder (Figure 3.21).

3.8.3 Body Fluids

Tunable light sources have long been used for the detection of biological fluids. Although they cannot be used to identify which type of fluid is present, they have been the mainstay for a forensic examiner attempting to locate biological evidence. Biological evidence can be detected using an FLS due to the inherent fluorescent properties of semen, saliva, vaginal secretions, urine, and sweat. Blood by contrast absorbs radiation extending from the UV into the IR, with the strongest absorption in the UV/blue-violet region of the electromagnetic spectrum

Most bodily fluids will respond to radiation from a UV source. However, depending on the supporting material, the background may fluoresce as well, minimizing any observable contrast in the subject. With a tunable wavelength source, the examiner may tune the wavelength of light and change barrier filters to minimize background fluorescence. The purpose is to induce fluorescence from the stain or enhance the contrast of the stain against a background. The fluorescence emission is typically much less intense

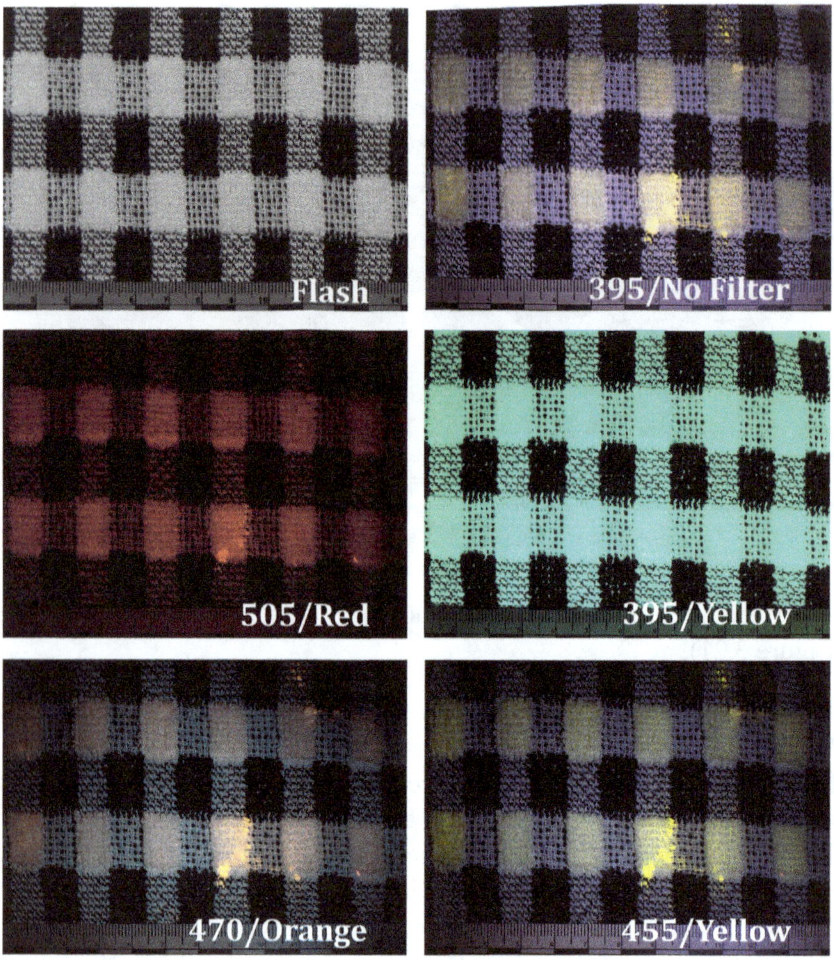

Figure 3.22 Varying degrees of success to visualize saliva stains on a checkered dishtowel using different excitation and barrier filters. The illumination and barrier filter (if any) is indicated on each image.

than the excitation radiation, making the proper wavelength/barrier filter selection critical for both visualization and photographic documentation.

The color of the fluorescent stain recorded by the camera will be a function of the colored barrier filter placed over the lens of the camera. Figure 3.22 depicts a saliva stain on black and white-checkered dishtowel that was photographed with different combinations of wavelengths and barrier filters. Different barrier filter and wavelength combinations

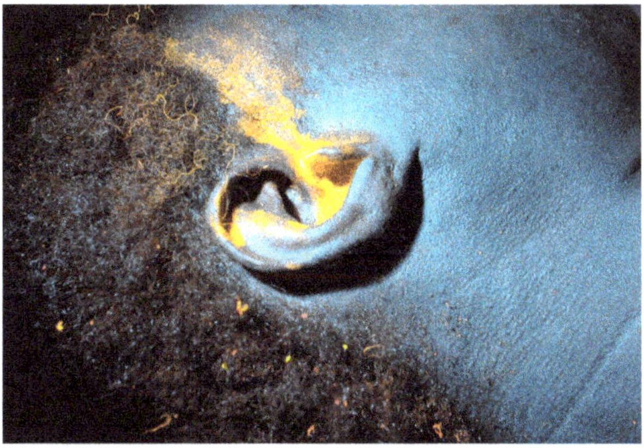

Figure 3.23 The orange colored fluorescent stain was collected for serological and DNA testing. The stain tested positive for amylase. Images were recorded with a Nikon D3x camera with the following exposure settings: f5.6, *10 seconds, and ISO 800.*

were use to help suppress the background fluorescence attributed to the white fibers.

Figure 3.23 depicts a decedent at autopsy with a stain surrounding the right ear. The image was taken with the SPEX HandScope set to "CSS" and an orange barrier filter placed over the camera lens.

Figure 3.24 depicts semen stains on white hand towel. The bottom image was taken with a Nikon D100 camera using 505 nm illumination and an orange barrier filter.

Blood is the most common physiological fluid encountered at crime scenes, and as previously mentioned has strong absorption in the near-UV and blue-violet regions. Since blood has strong absorption characteristics, it will appear dark. Contrast can be created between the bloodstains and its substrate if the background reflects or absorbs the radiation relative to the bloodstains or if the background is actively fluorescent.

The authors had a homicide case where the decedent's wife was accused of shooting her husband, three times, in the head at close range with a firearm belonging to the deceased. No blood or tissue was found on the weapon. In fact the weapon was pristine but exhibited signs of corrosion on some metal surfaces. It was hypothesized that the weapon was cleaned after the shooting with a corrosive chemical. A toolmark comparison conducted by a ballistics unit concluded that the recovered

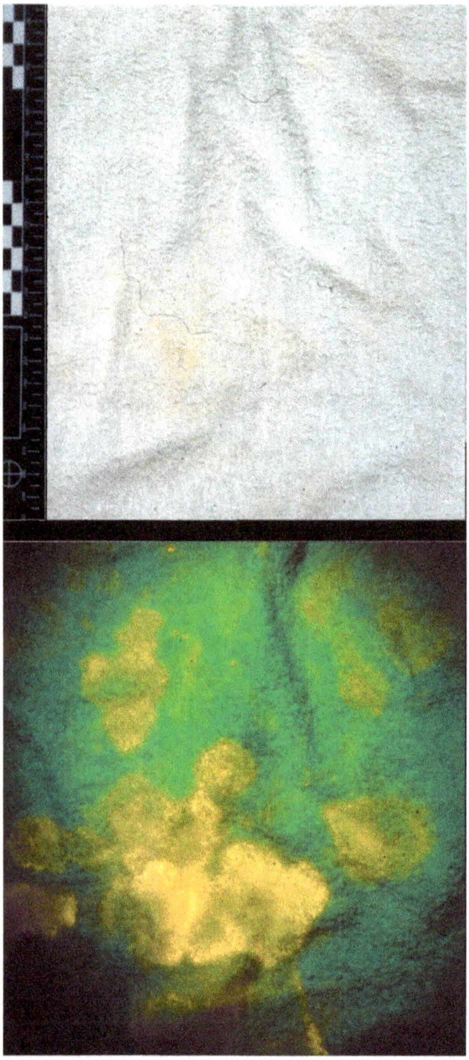

Figure 3.24 Fluorescent semen stains on a white hand towel.

bullets were fired from the decease's weapon. Investigators recovered a load of laundry in the dryer and a load of laundry still wet in the washing machine. It was also reported that an odor of bleach was detected from the washing machine. In examining this evidence, the objective was to try to locate any stains consistent with blood on the laundered garments. Having not encountered this circumstance before, and with little information garnered from a literature search of peer-reviewed scientific periodicals, a series of experiments were designed. Seven 100% white cotton shirts were spattered and dripped with defibrinated sheep blood and allowed dry at 10-minute intervals from time zero up to 1 hour. The bloodstained shirts were then laundered in a household washer and dryer with bleach and laundry detergent added to the wash cycle. The washing machine was run with cold water as heat can fix bloodstains to the substrate. An eighth shirt, unstained, was washed under the same washing conditions prior to the bloodstained shirts to serve as a negative control. The images in Figure 3.25A–D illustrate the results of these experiments.

After the washing and drying, some faint brown stains could be seen on the shirts. The shirts were next examined with the ALS. It was determined that the best contrast was achieved with 430 nm illumination and a yellow barrier filter. Contrast was created because the background fluoresced and the bloodstains absorbed the radiation and appeared dark. In fact much of the original pattern could be visualized. The sensitivity of detecting dilute bloodstains with ALS was also investigated. One drop, 25 microliters of serial diluted blood from 10^{-1} to 10^{-7}, was placed on Whatman® filter paper and allowed to dry. A negative control consisting of only distilled water was also used. The results are depicted in Figure 3.26. The limit of sensitivity using the ALS at 430 nm with a yellow barrier filter was approximately a 1:1000 dilution (10^{-3}). That is approximately the equivalent of one drop of blood in 1 oz of water. After the 1:1000 dilution, there was no visual difference detected with the ALS between the negative control and any subsequent dilutions.

3.8.4 Bloodstains and Chemiluminescence

Chemical testing was also performed on the laundered clothing mentioned in the previous case example. Because the bloodstains were already dilute and some of them could not be seen with the naked eye, luminol was chosen as a presumptive test. Luminol is a very sensitive chemical that reacts with blood to produce a blue-colored chemiluminescence. Chemical luminescence is a chemical reaction that produces light. The observation and photographic documentation of the chemiluminescence must take place in a darkened environment because the luminescence is weak and is not easily detected in an ambient light environment. Shutter speeds can vary, but usually should not exceed 30 seconds; the chemiluminescent reaction starts to diminish significantly after 30 seconds. The camera must be placed on a tripod and it is recommended to use a shutter

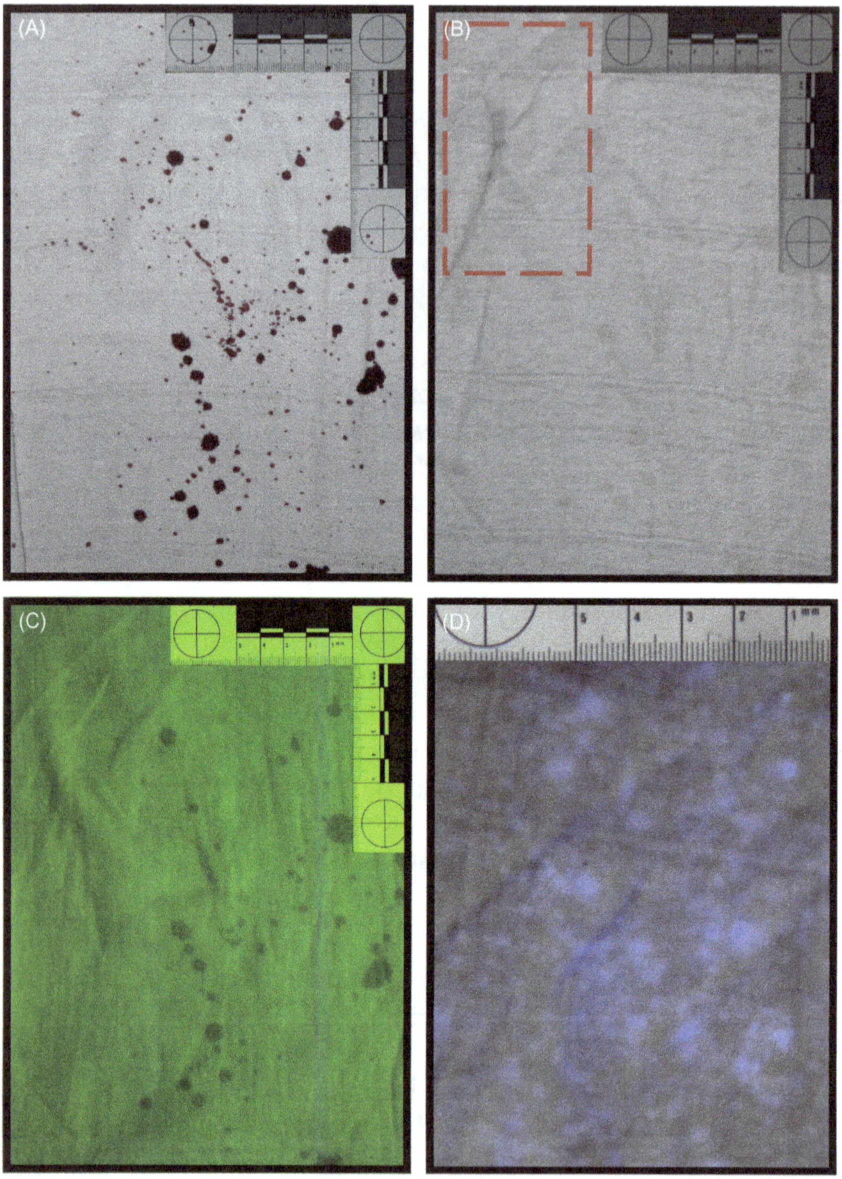

Figure 3.25 (A) Bloodstains on white 100% cotton. The bloodstain pattern was allowed to dry for a period of 30 minutes prior to being laundered. (B) The same shirt as in (A) after being laundered, recorded with normal flash photography. The only residual evidence of the bloodstains was the appearance of several faint brown stains. The highlighted area in red was the region chemically treated with luminol, which appears in (D). (C) Laundered shirt photographed with 430 nm illumination and a yellow barrier filter over the camera lens. Compared to (A), much of the original pattern can be visualized with the ALS. Image recorded with a Nikon D200 camera using the following exposure settings: f4.5, 20 seconds, and ISO 100. (D) The section of the laundered shirt that was highlighted in (B) was treated with luminol. No pattern could be recognized; this only provided an indication that blood could be present. The negative control did not react to the luminol.

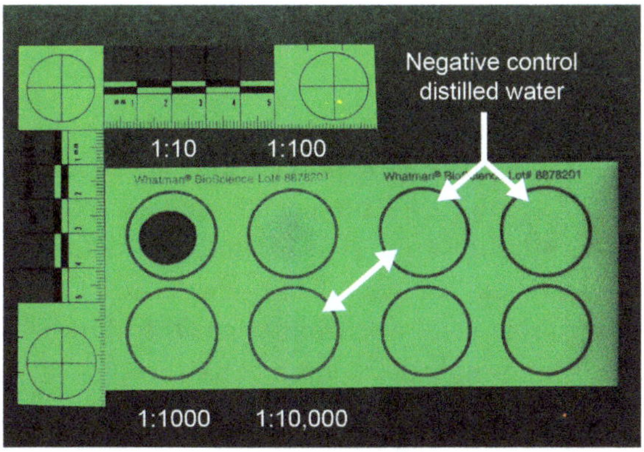

Figure 3.26 The sensitivity for the detection of dilute bloodstains using 430 nm illumination and a yellow barrier filter. After a blood dilution of 1:1000, no visual difference could be detected compared with the negative control. Image recorded with a Nikon D200 camera using the following exposure settings: f*4.5, 20 seconds, and ISO 100.*

release cable or a timer delay to avoid camera vibrations. The following guidelines serve as a good starting point for luminol photography:

- The camera is set up and secured to the tripod.
- First, manually focus in ambient light or first autofocus, and then move the selector to manual focus. The camera autofocus will not work properly in a completely darkened room.
- The exposure setting could be manual or aperture priority depending the accuracy of the aperture priority in low light environments.
- A typical manual exposure starting point would be
  - Aperture: *f*5.6
  - Shutter speed: 30 seconds
  - ISO: 100
  - Rear curtain flash.

A rear curtain flash is a camera setting that should be found on any quality DSLR camera. With the rear curtain flash selected, the flash fires as the shutter is about to close, as opposed to when it first opens. A sync cord should be used to remove the flash from the camera. The exposure compensation on the flash should be lowered to underexpose the image. The flash should also be directed at the ceiling or a corner of the room away from the evidence. Doing so, the illumination from the flash is bounced off a wall or ceiling and provides just enough illumination to visualize the background without overwhelming the chemiluminescence. Photographing luminol in this manner is critical for placing any possible bloodstains detected in context with the crime scene or evidence.

Figure 3.27 gives another illustration of luminol photography. In a homicide case, the victim was assaulted and stabbed by a roommate. Subsequent to the assault, the subject in the case removed his bloodstained clothing and showered. The bathroom of the homicide scene was carefully examined for bloodstain evidence. Faint, visible, and dilute red/brown stains were apparent when the shower was examined with light from a high-intensity source. The shower was systematically processed with luminol, small sections at a time. The camera was set up and focused prior to spraying the chemical; after the lights were turned off, the chemical was sprayed and the shutter opened. A positive luminol reaction was observed on the floor of the shower as depicted in Figure 3.27.

When using luminol, a systematic testing approached is critical to proper documentation. It is important to set up the camera equipment prior to any treatment with luminol because the initial chemiluminescent reaction will have the highest luminous intensity. Subsequent treatments of an area that already contains dilute blood

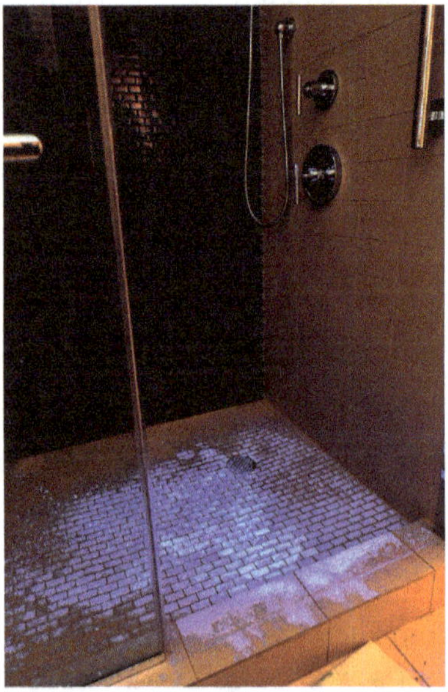

Figure 3.27 Chemiluminescence with luminol recorded with a Nikon D3x camera using the following exposure settings: f5.6, 25 seconds, ISO 200, and an exposure compensated (for under exposure) rear curtain flash.

with luminol will only dilute that blood further, and the luminous intensity of the reaction will rapidly decrease as blood is diluted past the sensitivity limits of the reagent.

3.8.5 Document Examination

Writing and printing inks that have a high organic content formulation can be induced to fluoresce in the visible spectrum with short wavelength radiation. Official government documents such as passports, monetary bills, and drivers' licenses can have holograms printed with fluorescent inks or invisible markings that fluoresce with shortwave (UV/blue-violet) radiation. These security features are designed to deter forgeries.

Figure 3.28A shows a photograph of the back of an official New York State driver's license recorded with normal flash photography. The fluorescent "NY" markings observed in Figure 3.28B could not be visualized with normal flash photography or with oblique, white light, illumination.

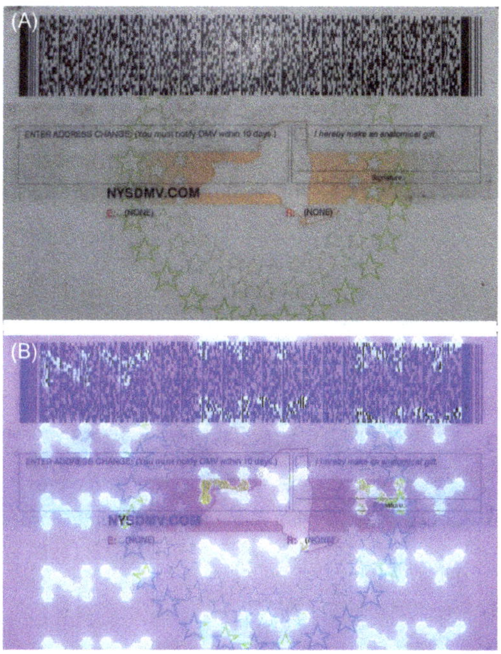

Figure 3.28 Fluorescent printing on the back of an official New York State driver's license. Bottom image recorded with a Nikon Coolpix P100 camera and 365 nm illumination with the following exposure settings: f4.0, 8 seconds, ISO 200, and no filter over the camera lens.

Certain denominations of modern US currency (*circa* 1990) have a thin vertical strip of fabric woven into the note about 25 mm from the left edge. In Figure 3.29, printed on the fluorescent strip for the $20 denomination appears the notation "USA TWENTY 20." The currency note was illuminated with near-UV illumination (365 nm), in a darkroom, and with no filter over the camera lens. Not only does the fabric strip fluoresce but the printing inks also appear dramatically different under UV radiation.

3.8.6 Paint and Cleaning Agents

Architectural paint can be used to conceal physical evidence of a crime committed. Several articles describe the use of tunable light sources and reflected IR photography to detect bloodstain pattern evidence

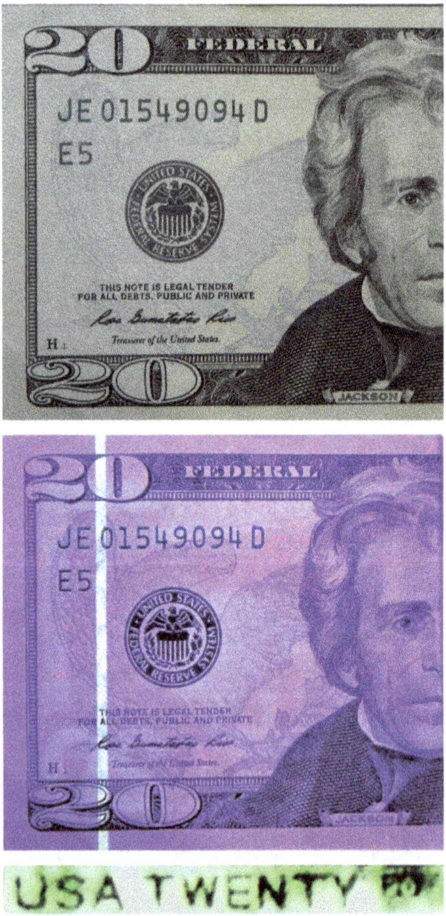

Figure 3.29 Fluorescent markings on a $20 denomination of US currency.

beneath painted surfaces. Art conservators use these techniques to detect alterations and restorations or to reveal drawings or markings beneath painted surfaces of works of art. In the following case example, the decedent was stabbed to death in an apartment. In a vain attempt to conceal the commission of a crime, the apartment was freshly painted, and even the bathtub was hand painted a battleship gray color. Despite the cleanup attempt, bloodstains were readily visible throughout the apartment. Figure 3.30A depicts an area of the apartment near the bathroom. The walls were examined with a tunable light source. Graffiti was revealed in several locations beneath painted surfaces. Figure 3.30B depicts the wall to the left of a dresser illuminated with a SPEX instrument set to CSS and photographed using an orange barrier filter. Along with the graffiti, fluorescent orange rivulets can also be visualized in the image, the residue left from a cleaning agent.

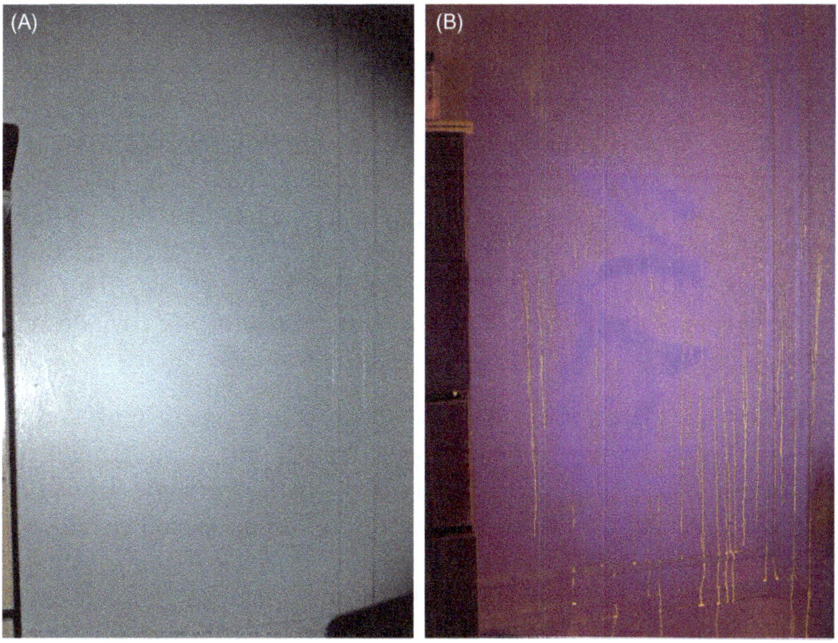

Figure 3.30 (A) Photograph taken of a wall within a residence where a homicide occurred. In an attempt to hide evidence of the homicide, the apartment was painted to conceal blood. The photograph was taken with a Nikon D200 camera on a tripod and the wall was illuminated with white light from a high-intensity tunable source. (B) Wall area to the left of the dresser, depicted in (A), illuminated with broadband blue-green light and an orange barrier filter showing graffiti beneath paint and fluorescence from cleaning agents. Image photographed with a Nikon D200 camera using the following exposure settings: f3.5, 4.5 seconds, and ISO 200.

CHAPTER 4

Digital Infrared Photography

The effectiveness of forensic infrared (IR) photography lies in the ability to create contrast on difficult to manage or dark backgrounds. An example of this would be the visualization of gunshot residue on a bloodstained, black-colored fabric. Objects that appear similar in color with the unaided eye may appear completely different in IR. *Infrared* simply means the part of the electromagnetic spectrum that is longer in wavelength than red. As discussed earlier, the classification of electromagnetic radiation by wavelength is called the electromagnetic spectrum. Our eyes can only perceive the visible light portion of the electromagnetic spectrum. However, digital cameras and film emulsions are sensitive to the ultraviolet (UV, radiation shorter than blue-violet light) and IR.

One of the popular misconceptions of IR photography is the visualization of heat escaping from windows and doorways lacking proper insulation. This type of IR imaging is commonly referred to as thermography, or thermal imaging, an imaging technique in which an IR camera is used to measure temperature variations on surfaces. Ironically, the sensitivity of IR photographic films and digital single-lens reflex (DSLR) cameras does not come anywhere near the part of the energy spectrum emitted by heat escaping through windows or doors.

IR is usually divided into three spectral regions: near-, mid- and far-IR, and ranges roughly from 700 to 1000 nm (1 μm) in wavelength. The boundaries between the near-, mid-, and far-IR regions are not finite and can vary slightly depending on the information source. Between roughly 700 and 3000 nm is referred to as the near-IR. The full spectrum of IR is not used for DSLR IR photography. Camera sensors are sensitive from about 350 to 1000 nm. Therefore, the same recording techniques for NIR can be used for visible light observations, with the exception for observation by the naked eye. The IR radiation documented in a photograph is the measure of the amount of near-IR radiation reflected or absorbed by the subject. If an object absorbs IR radiation,

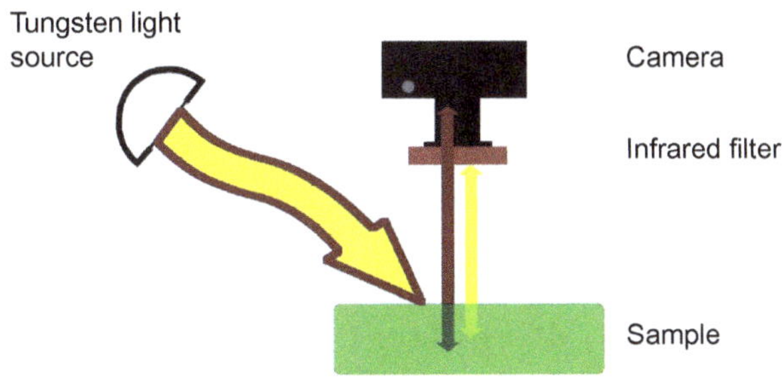

Figure 4.1 Illustration of a basic setup for IR photography.

it will appear dark in the image. If an object reflects IR radiation, it will appear bright in the image. IR photography works in much the same way our eyes perceive colored objects. The human eye and brain interpret a red apple to be "red" because the apple absorbs the separate colors (radiation) that compose the visible light spectrum. The red portion of the visible light spectrum is reflected from the apple into our eyes, which the brain perceives as "red."

The typical IR photographic setup is illustrated in Figure 4.1. A source rich in IR radiation is used to irradiate the physical evidence. The IR radiation can be reflected or absorbed by the subject. An opaque filter is placed over the camera lens that only transmits near-IR radiation and blocks visible light.

An alternative to the setup previously described involves the use of a forensic light source that is filtered to emit only IR radiation to illuminate the subject. In this layout, no filter is necessary over the camera lens, provided the photography has taken place in a darkroom with the lights off.

4.1 DIGITAL IR PHOTOGRAPHY

4.1.1 Cameras and Specialized Photographic Equipment

The obvious advantage of digital imaging is the function of instant analysis, particularly while working with difficult subjects as is often encountered with forensic photography. The transition to digital imaging from the traditional emulsion-based photography has stimulated a renewed interest in IR photography. IR films were typically sensitive and difficult to handle. IR films do not have an antihalation backing, which prevents radiation from being reflected by the pressure plate. If the pressure plate has a pronounced pattern, there is a chance that you see the same pattern on the negatives, the so-called ghost image or halo effect. This also means the film is very susceptible to fogging and must be handled in absolute darkness.

Digital cameras have image sensors, called charge-coupled devices (CCDs). Another common type of sensor is the complementary metal-oxide semiconductor (CMOS) sensor that records the image. All digital cameras have a filter or "hot mirror" in front of the image sensor. The purpose of the filter is to allow visible light to be recorded on the sensor, forming the image, while blocking UV and IR radiation from being recorded. If too much UV radiation is recorded in the image, the blue hues appear as deeper blue. If too much IR radiation is recorded in the image, the red hues appear as darker red. The true purpose of the hot mirror is to allow for a faithful and accurate color rendition of the scene or subject.

To some extent, any digital camera can record near-IR radiation regardless of the hot mirror in front of the image sensor. Camera models can have different hot mirrors, so each camera type differs in sensitivity to IR radiation. These types of filters are not perfect but are getting more efficient. There is inherently a small amount of "leakage." That is to say, a small amount of near-IR radiation does pass through the filter. Some camera models such as the Canon PowerShot G series marketed prior to 2004 were known to pass a significant amount of IR radiation.

A camera such as the PowerShot G1 and a deep red filter such as the Hoya R72 were all that were needed to start taking IR images. The Nikon D70 and D70s also transmit a fair amount of IR radiation and have been popular choices for an "off-the-shelf" digital SLR IR camera.

It is easy to verify if a digital camera is capable of recording IR radiation. Point a television remote at the lens of a digital camera while depressing any button on the remote. At the same time, depress the shutter release button on the camera recording the image (Figure 4.2). Standard remote controls use IR radiation to signal the television; if your digital camera is capable of recording IR radiation, the light-emitting diode (LED) at the front of the remote will appear as a bright dot in your image.

Imaging sensors only record the intensity of the radiation striking the photosensitive device. Placing a blue, green, and red color filter

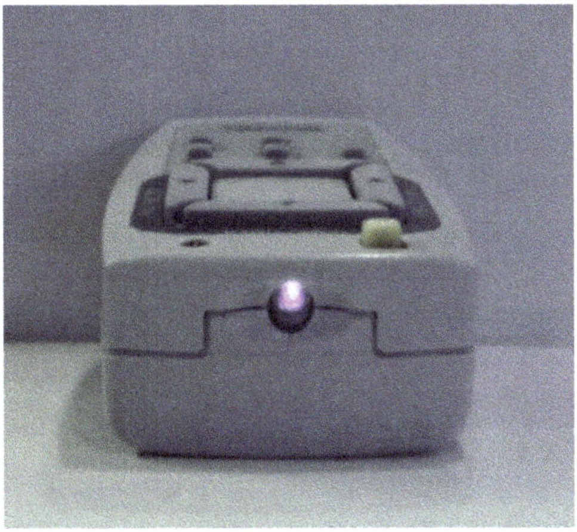

Figure 4.2 The IR signal from a remote control. The image was recorded with an off-the-shelf Nikon Coolpix P100. The camera was mounted on a copy stand with the following settings: f8, 1/7 seconds, and ISO 160. The image was also recorded with ambient illumination. No flash was used.

array over the camera sensor produces visible light color images. The filter array allows the camera to interpret color from the sensor data. IR radiation does not carry any color information and is only a measure of the intensity of the IR radiation reflected off a subject. Since IR carries no color information, the appearance should be monochrome. The term monochrome is usually taken to mean grayscale, but may also be used to refer to various tones of a single color. If the IR filter blocks all visible light, then the image will be grayscale, provided a manual white balance has been correctly performed. Colored IR images, depending on the cut-on filter used, are a result of some visible light reaching the sensor. Colors can also be enhanced or modified using postproduction software applications.

4.1.2 Specialized Cameras

Typically, a visibly opaque filter is fitted over the camera lens to block any visible light from reaching the sensor when taking an IR image. With an unmodified camera, this opaque filter combined with the hot mirror in front of the sensor allows for very little radiation to reach the sensor. This results in poor quantum efficiency of the photosensitive device necessitating the use of a tripod and long exposure times and makes composing a shot with sharp focus very difficult. These cameras are generally not suitable for IR photography. Cameras can be modified to work with a much greater sensitivity to IR radiation.

Two solutions will be discussed to this problem that centers on the hot mirror; both require the filter to be removed. The first solution is to convert a DSLR to a stand-alone IR camera. To accomplish this, the camera's internal hot mirror must be removed and replaced with a cut-on, longpass filter that only transmits IR radiation. The advantage to this arrangement is that it allows for handheld shots with normal exposure times at low ISO (International Organization for Standardization) and autofocus use, and the cameras viewfinder can still be used. The replacement filter over the sensor should have a cut-on wavelength near 650 nm. IR filters can be placed over the lens that have longer cut-on wavelengths when there is a need to work deeper into the IR spectrum. If a filter is placed over the lens, this will negate the use of the viewfinder and likely the autofocus.

The second solution is to convert a DSLR camera to a full-spectrum camera that can effectively record UV, visible light, and IR radiation. In this conversion, the hot mirror is replaced by a material that is capable of transmitting radiation through the UV, visible, and IR regions of the electromagnetic spectrum such as quartz Fujifilm developed the FinePix S3 Pro UVIR full-spectrum DSLR camera and unveiled it in 2005. An added benefit of this camera was that it had been designed to be compatible with Nikon accessories. Unfortunately, this camera was marketed primarily to the forensic science industry and has since been discontinued. With any full-spectrum camera, external filters need to be mounted over the lens to facilitate taking pictures with UV, visible light, or IR radiation. Any camera with the hot mirror filter removed can be used in the visible light range if a filter with the same properties as a hot mirror is used on the lens.

There are Internet sites with step-by-step tutorials for do-it-yourself IR conversion kits. It is recommended that if you are considering conversion of a DLSR camera to an IR camera, seek out an insured professional to do so.

4.1.3 Light Sources

An important aspect of scientific photography is the ability to photograph evidence under controlled illumination. Choosing the correct source rich in IR radiation is important. There are many light sources used in photography that are also found in forensic laboratories that are rich in IR radiation. Daylight and ambient illumination cannot readily be controlled and are often unwanted in scientific photography. There is a need to control the type of illumination and the angle of incidence in order to obtain a satisfactory and forensically useful image.

Incandescent sources, such a household light bulb with a tungsten filament or photoflood lamps, operate based on the emission of electromagnetic radiation (visible and IR) from a filament as the result of increase in its temperature. Incandescence produces visible light but much of the energy output is in the IR portion of the electromagnetic spectrum. A tungsten filament lamp is a useful source for the wavelength region between 350 and 2500 nm.

In addition to the sources that depend on the heating of materials, there are some that depend on an electric discharge through gases sealed in a glass tube. There are many such sources, but some, like fluorescent tubes used for room lighting, are not suitable for IR work. Fluorescent tubes and high-intensity discharge lights, typically used to illuminate parking lots, are considered discrete sources and emit relatively little IR energy.

Modern electronic flash units contain a tube filled with xenon gas, where an electric current is used to generate an electrical arc that creates a short burst of light. These flash units are also a rich source of IR radiation. However, flash units will not work properly unless the camera has been modified for IR imaging.

Many high-intensity, tunable wavelength light sources also employ a xenon arc source. These systems operate by utilizing a series of stepped interference filters, which are then tunable by tilting their angle to the light beam to give a continuously variable output from 300 to 1000 nm. Units such as the CrimeScope CS-16 have an IR port with an accessory light guide where interchangeable IR filters can be mounted on the head of the light guide to illuminate the subject.

LED as alternate light sources have gained a foothold in the forensics industry primarily because they are less cumbersome to carry and are more energy efficient. These flashlight-type units use interchangeable LED heads that can be purchased in variety of wavelength bands including UV and IR.

4.1.4 Filters

There are many uses of filtration techniques in forensic science. The purpose of a filter is to block certain wavelengths of radiation while allowing transmission of selected wavelengths.

This discussion on filters will be limited to the filters used over the camera lens for IR photography. These filters fall into a category known as longpass, cut-on filters. They transmit nearly 100% of the near-IR radiation but rapidly decrease to 0% transmittance as the wavelength of radiation approaches 700 nm (deep red). Such filters block visible light and transmit the IR radiation reflected off the subject.

IR filters are visibly opaque and are very difficult or impossible to see through. There are a number of companies that manufacture filters for IR photography such as Peca, Hoya, Tiffen, B + W, Heliopan, Schott, and Kodak. Each filter manufacturer has a coded mark printed on the side of the filter ring. The code indicates which wavelength regions the filter transmits. Unfortunately, there is no industry standard for these codes and they vary from manufacturer to manufacturer (Table 4.1). This can very easily lead to confusion for those who are not familiar with these kinds of filters.

Cut-on wavelength is a term used to denote the wavelength at which the transmission increases to 50% throughput in a longpass

Table 4.1 Various IR Filters and Their Equivalents

Wratten	Peca	Schott	B + W	Hoya	Tiffen	0%T (nm)	50%T (nm)
#25	–	OG590	090	25A	25	510	590
#29	–	RG630	091	–	29	540	630
#70	902	RG665	–	–	–	580	665
#89B	914	RG695	092	R72	–	610	695
#88A	912	RG715	–	–	–	620	715
#87	904	RG780	–	–	87	610	780
#87C	910	RG830	093	–	–	670	830
#87B	908	RG850	–	RM90	–	700	850
#87A	906	RG1000	094	RM100	–	730	1000

Percent transmission (%T) values are based on published data for Schott filters. Precise values may vary slightly depending on the manufacturer.

filter. For example, for the Peca 914 and its equivalent the Hoya R72, the cut-on wavelength is 720 nm. So at 50% maximum transmission, the corresponding wavelength value for that filter is 720 nm.

To add another layer of confusion to filter nomenclature, not all manufacturers use the 50% transmission value to denote the cut-on wavelength. The wavelength at 0% or 5% transmission can also be used to denote the transition from a region of low transmission to an adjacent region of high spectral transmission. The 0% or 5% designation will always have a shorter wavelength than the 50% value for longpass filters. For example, the equivalent of the Kodak Wratten #89B has a 5% transmission at 690 nm (deep red) and at 50% transmission, the value is 720 nm (near-IR). Usually with longpass filters, at 5%T the slope of the transmission curve starts to increase rapidly, indicating a region of high transmission. For IR photography purposes, the 0%T or 5%T value is more practical; it gives the photographer a better understanding of how much visible red will be transmitted through the filter and recorded in the image.

IR filters fall into three basic categories: filters that let in some visible (red) light, filters that transmit very little visible light, and filters that transmit zero visible light (Figure 4.3). Although there are a variety of filters available from various manufacturers, you can get away with the use of only three filters. One filter from each of the basic categories should suffice for forensic subject matters. Quality filters can cost several hundreds of dollars apiece. If you are just getting started and want to experiment with IR photography, there are cheap alternatives. Unexposed but developed 35 mm slide film or the disk from a

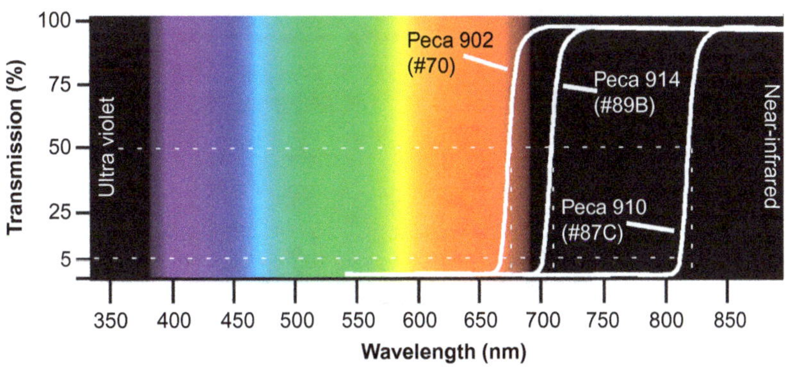

Figure 4.3 Transmission curves for three IR filters with different cut-on wavelengths.

3.5″ floppy (removed from the plastic housing) placed over the camera lens can serve as an effective IR filter. These materials block most visible radiation and transmit some IR radiation.

Figure 4.4 illustrates the effects these filters have on a multicolored fleece fabric. As the cut-on wavelength goes deeper into the IR, the colors and pattern of the fabric begin to drop out. When all the visible

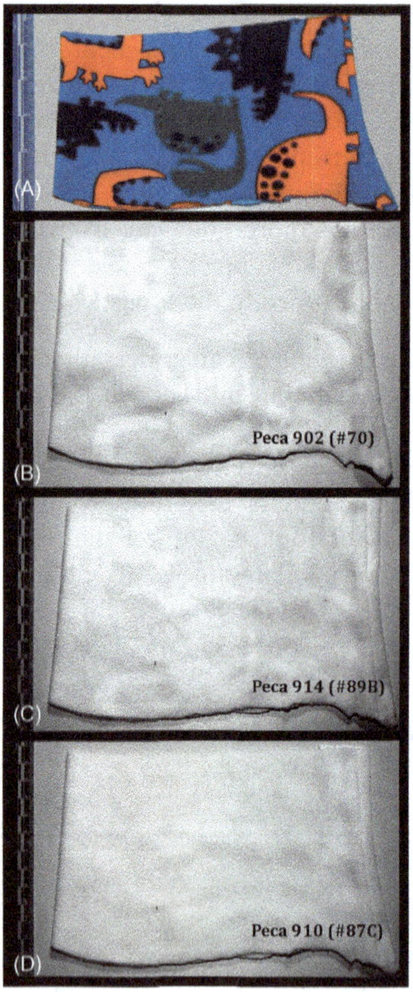

Figure 4.4 (A) 100% polyester fleece recorded with normal flash photography. (B–D) Subsequent images recorded with IR photography using Fuji FinePix S3 Pro and the indicated IR filter at f11, 1/60 seconds, ISO 400, and flash illumination. As the cut-on wavelength for the respective filter progresses deeper into the near-IR, the pattern is progressively removed.

light is completely blocked with the Peca 910 (#87C), the pattern has been completely dropped from the fabric.

4.1.5 Photographic Considerations

Digital IR photography necessitates the need for a specialized camera, a selection of longpass, cut-on filters, a light source rich in IR radiation that can be easily controlled, and a copy stand or quality tripod. A remote shutter release cable is also recommended to reduce vibrations and camera movement. There are also technical controls on the camera that need to be adjusted prior to shooting in the IR.

4.1.5.1 White Balance

For IR photography, it is necessary to perform a custom white balance in order to obtain the correct color temperature for the filter/light source combination being used. The automatic white balance (AWB) set on a modified IR camera with the IR filter in place results in the saturation of the red color channel. Depending on the type of filter used, the image will have a pronounced reddish or purple cast with AWB.

Traditional black and white photography requires the use of an 18% gray card to set the white balance depending on color temperature of the light source. With IR photography, an object must be chosen that adequately reflects IR radiation to set the white balance. Nature photographers have used green grass or green foliage on a sunlit day to set the white balance because green vegetation reflects a great deal of IR radiation and appears white or neutral in the image. Foliage likely is not a practical subject to set the white balance in the laboratory or at a crime scene. It will be necessary to experiment with suitable surfaces for white balancing that reflect enough IR radiation so the image appears neutral. We have found that white, ceramic floor tile works well for this purpose.

The user should consult the manual for that specific camera to set a custom white balance. There can be complications to setting a custom white balance with IR photography. It may take several attempts to get a white balance within range. Cameras are set by the manufacturer to have a minimum and maximum color temperature range. It is recommended to operate the camera in manual mode and adjust the shutter speed until a suitable white balance is achieved.

4.1.5.2 File Format

Most cameras offer file formats in JPEG, RAW, and TIFF in older models. Many cameras now offer JPEG + RAW where both formats are recorded simultaneously. Even though RAW files are large and can occupy quite a bit of hard drive space, it is recommended that images be recorded in the RAW format for IR photography. If the images recorded are for examining quality analysis, then RAW offers a far superior image quality compared to JPEG. Post-processing image development is usually part of the digital IR workflow, and RAW offers many advantages postproduction. If your camera does not have a black and white mode, or you do not use black and white mode, the camera will record a "false color" image. Postproduction image development is necessary to render the false color image black and white or grayscale and to remedy any white balance or exposure issues.

4.1.5.3 International Organization for Standardization

For best image quality, it is ideal to set the ISO, the camera's sensitivity to radiation, as low as possible. A high ISO can introduce digital noise and give the image a grainy appearance. Emulsions used for IR photography were fast films because of the required long exposure times. Fast films have a grainy appearance; the advantage to digital IR photography is the ability to reduce this grainy appearance. The trade off to using a low ISO of course is longer shutter speeds. Mounting the camera on a stable tripod or copy stand and using a remote shutter release can reduce this noise associated with longer shutter speeds.

4.1.5.4 Lenses

There are many different kinds of lenses that can be used for IR photography. For forensic documentation purposes, typically, a macro or a variable focal length zoom lens will be used. Older lenses, e.g., the ones that were put away along with the 35 mm camera, can also be used. It would be worthwhile to reexamine older lenses that were put out of service to determine if there is an IR marking engraved on the barrel of the lens to correct for focus aberrations. Lens manufacturers typically have either a white or red dot or a red colored "R" near the central focus mark on the barrel of the lens to indicate the IR focus mark. Modern-day DSLR lenses no longer have the focusing mark to correct aberrations that occur with IR radiation.

What matters most is the optical quality of the lens. Good camera lenses are *achromatic*. They are designed to bring two colors, blue and green, into focus in one plane on the imaging sensor. *Apochromatic* lenses, sometimes called "APO," are chromatically corrected for three colors: blue, green, and red. With apochromatic lenses blue, green, and red will be focused in one plane. Many manufacturers market apochromatic lenses; however, some but not all of these lenses are only APO corrected at the center of the lens. Apochromatic lenses are more expensive; the advantage with IR photography is that a full apochromatic lens also brings IR radiation into focus when first focusing in visible light. Most photographers would not even notice the difference between an *achromatic* and *apochromatic* visible light photograph when examining them with the unaided eye.

4.1.5.5 Focus Shift

Focusing the image requires an adjustment to account for the difference in refraction of IR radiation and visible light. IR radiation is longer in wavelength than visible radiation and will come into focus beyond the imaging sensor, which has been positioned for the correction of two or three wavelengths of visible light (Figure 4.5). If the lens is fully apochromatic, then the IR radiation should be in focus even when focusing in visible light. When focusing with an achromatic lens in visible light, the IR radiation will be focused behind the image sensor. The IR filter is visibly opaque, and when positioned over the lens,

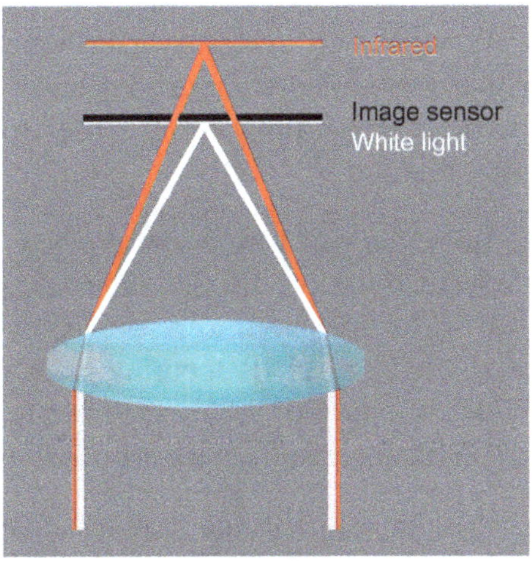

Figure 4.5 IR focus shift through a simple lens.

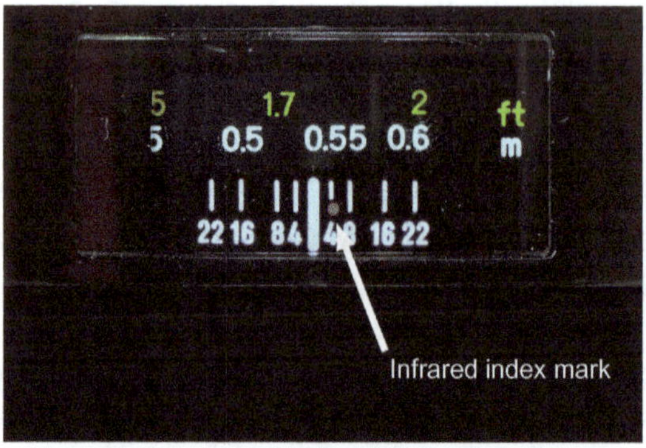

Figure 4.6 IR index mark on an older lens.

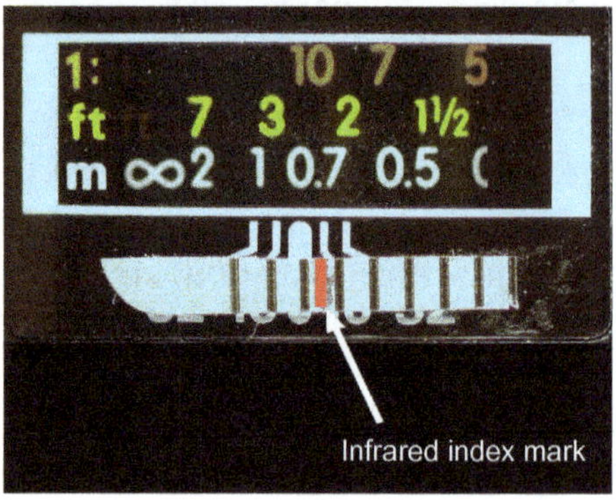

Figure 4.7 IR index mark on a calibrated lens using scale tape.

framing the subject will not be possible using the viewfinder. One way to circumvent this is to use an accessory viewfinder in the camera's accessory shoe or use a modified camera that has a "live view" function. Both of these accessories allow for the user to frame and focus the subject using IR radiation.

If the camera is not equipped with a live preview function, then the lens can be calibrated to bring the IR radiation into focus. In order to correct for this, the lens elements need to be moved by rotating the focus ring. If the lens being used has an IR focusing mark (Figure 4.6), focus normally with the filter is removed. Secure the filter to the lens, and then rotate the focus ring so the focused distance is opposite the index mark.

If the lens does not have an IR index mark, then it is possible to calibrate the lens. A narrow strip of scale tape can be cut and placed on the barrel of the lens near the central focusing mark (Figure 4.7).

A series of test shots can be made adjusting the focus in small increments after each subsequent shot. After reviewing the series of images, the scale tape can be marked accordingly corresponding to the image of best focus.

4.1.5.6 Aperture and Shutter Speed

For all practical purposes, it is best to work in manual mode to select the exposure setting. Although the camera's internal metering system is sensitive to IR radiation and will meter, the values are seldom accurate. Once you become more accustomed to imaging with IR and become more familiar with how your camera operates in the IR, it is possible to work in aperture or shutter priority modes.

Many photographers working in the IR chose to use high *f*-numbers (smaller aperture). Although this increases the exposure time, the added benefit is an increased depth of field that can help mitigate the focus shift problems.

Even with a modified camera, it may be necessary to bracket the exposure and take several shots in ± ½ stop increments to ensure a proper exposure. With image processing, it is always easier to work with an underexposed image than an overexposed image. Many a time, details can be recovered with an underexposed image using a software program that cannot be recovered with an overexposed image.

4.1.5.7 Resolution

When photographing with IR, one must be cognizant of a slight reduction in resolution when compared to the same visible light image. Even with optimal exposure settings, a low ISO and proper focus, on close inspection, the image may appear fuzzy. This is not to say that IR photographs produce a poor quality image with limited usefulness. It is only something to remain aware of if resolution is important (i.e., distinguishing between two closely spaced lines) and the emphasis is to purchase quality camera equipment. The reason for this can be explained by examining a simple resolution equation:

$$R = x(\lambda/NA) \tag{4.1}$$

where the resolution (R) can be approximated by multiplying a constant x (usually taken to be 0.5 or 0.61) by the wavelength of light (λ) divided by the numerical aperture (NA) of the lens. It can be seen that given a specific lens, as wavelength increases, resolution decreases. Conversely, as wavelength decreases, resolution increases. Resolution can be increased, where the resolution value indicates the smallest resolvable distance between two lines, by using a large numerical aperture lens and shorter wavelengths of light.

4.2 FORENSIC APPLICATIONS OF IR PHOTOGRAPHY

4.2.1 Bloodstain Patterns

The applications of digital IR photography are varied and largely depend on the knowledge of the properties of the sample being photographed and the properties of the substrate onto which that sample is deposited. For example, a bloodstain pattern on a white ceramic floor tile would not be photographed very well in the IR. Although blood does absorb some IR radiation, the reflected IR radiation from the tile overwhelms the blood and makes it appear transparent. In Figure 4.8, when the floor tile is photographed in the IR, the thinner contact transfers appear transparent, while the thicker droplets are still visible.

That is not to say bloodstains are not a useful subject matter for IR photography. The effect of photographing bloodstains with IR radiation largely depends on the physical properties of the substrate and the thickness of the stain. Bloodstains deposited on dark fabrics or fabrics with a complex pattern can oftentimes be better visualized with IR

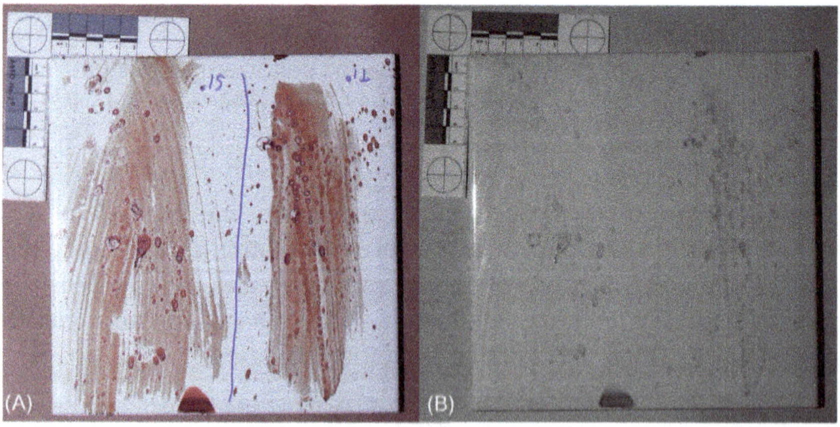

Figure 4.8 Contact transfers and blood spatter deposited on white ceramic floor tile. (A) Photographed under controlled lighting conditions. (B) photographed using IR radiation with the Fuji FinePix S3 Pro, f8, 1/60 seconds, flash, ISO 100, and #87C filter. The thinner contact transfers appear transparent, but the thicker blood droplets are still visible.

photography. If enough of the IR radiation is reflected off the substrate, the fabric will appear white or neutral. Blood contains several components, lipids, hemoglobin, and other proteins, that absorb IR radiation and will appear dark in an IR image. This results in dark stains on a significantly lighter background (Figures 4.9 and 4.10).

With fabrics, the dye does not contribute significantly to the effect visualized in an IR photograph. Compared by weight, the dye is a very small percentage of the total weight of the fabric. Whether a fabric absorbs or reflects IR radiation is a direct result of the chemical properties of the fibers. IR radiation will also penetrate the surface of materials to greater degree than white light or UV radiation. The sequence of images in Figures 4.11A–C happened rather accidentally. Fabric from a pair of 100% polyester, black-colored dress pants was secured to a cardboard backing for a research experiment. Bloodstains were

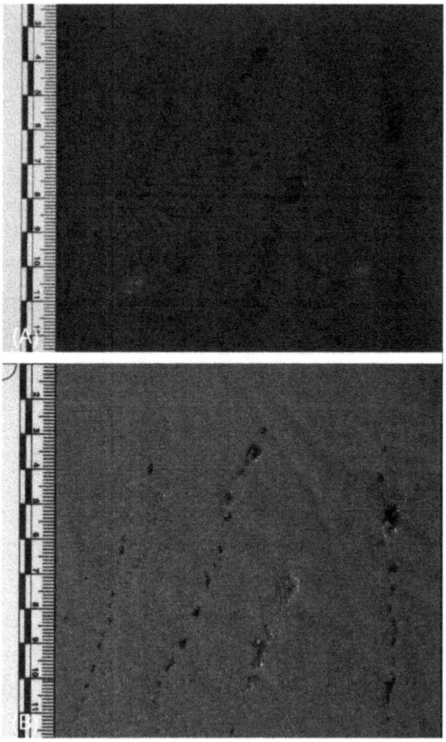

Figure 4.9 Bloodstains deposited onto a dark blue colored, 100% nylon, water-resistant fabric. (A) Photographed using normal flash photography. (B) Photographed using IR radiation with the Fuji FinePix S3 Pro with the following camera settings: f4.8, 1/250 seconds, ISO 400, incandescent illumination, and Peca 914 (#89B) filter.

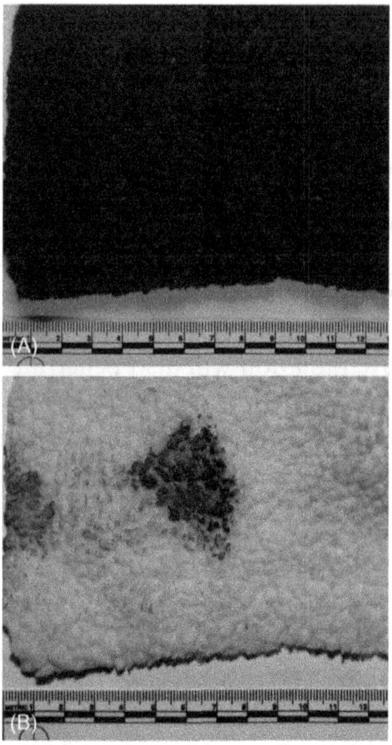

Figure 4.10 Bloodstains deposited onto a brown colored, 100% polyester fleece fabric. (A) Photographed using normal flash photography. (B) Photographed using IR radiation with the Fuji FinePix S3 Pro with the following camera settings: f4.8, 1/250 seconds, ISO 400, incandescent illumination, and Peca 914 (#89B) filter.

deposited onto the fabric and allowed to dry completely. Normal flash photographs as well as IR photographs were taken. After reviewing the IR photographs, the printing on the cardboard underneath the fabric could be visualized.

4.2.2 Gunshot Residue

IR photography can also be used for the visualization of gunshot residues on dark surfaces or on bloodstained clothing. The particulates and smoke that are expelled from the end of the barrel as well as the bullet wipe deposited around the rim of the entrance hole absorb IR strongly. In some instances, depending on the substrate, the gunshot residue can be visualized with IR photography on difficult backgrounds.

Figure 4.12 depicts a bullet entrance hole in a boot. The entrance hole is at the seam where the toecap meets the toe vamp. Both areas

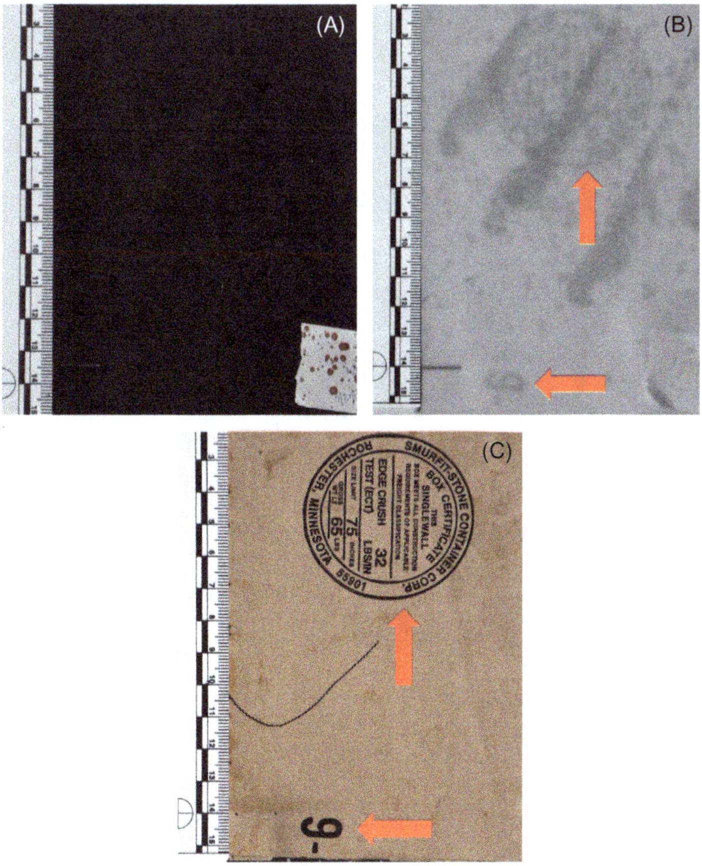

Figure 4.11 (A) Normal flash photograph of bloodstained polyester fabric secured with staples to a cardboard substrate. (B) IR image of the same black fabric; arrows indicate the printing on the cardboard under the fabric that could be visualized with IR radiation. Image recorded with the Fuji FinePix S3 Pro with exposure settings f4.8, 1/250 seconds, ISO 400, incandescent illumination, and Peca 914 (#89B) filter. (C) Normal flash photography of the cardboard substrate illustrating the printing on the cardboard.

are black in color providing photographic contrast problems in white light. Even though the parts of the shoe are visually similar in color, they are composed of different materials. In the IR, the vamp and the stitching reflect IR radiation and appear white creating contrast between the bullet hole, toecap, and vamp.

Blood can be described as semitransparent in the near-IR, whereas gunshot residue is a strong absorber of IR radiation. Due to the difference in absorption and reflection of IR radiation the blood will appear lighter compared to the gunshot residue, creating contrast. IR

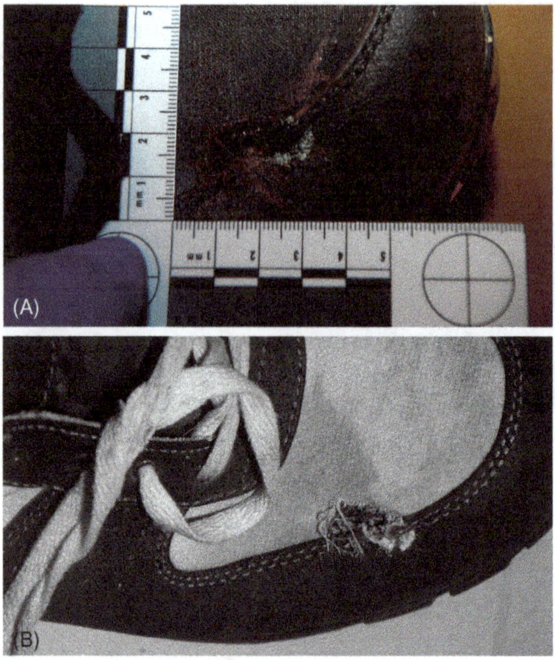

Figure 4.12 (A) Normal flash photograph illustrating the lack of contrast between the bullet entrance hole and the toe of the boot. (B) An IR photograph captured using the Fuji FinePix S3 Pro with the following exposure settings: f8.0, 1/60 seconds, ISO 200, flash illumination, and the Peca 914 (#89B) filter.

photography can be used to essentially "see through" the bloodstains in order to visualize the gunshot residue on a bloodstained fabric (Figure 4.13).

IR photography is also very useful for visualizing gunshot residue (GSR) on deeply pigmented individuals. Skin tones photographed under IR radiation take on a milk glass or white porcelain appearance especially with dark-skinned individuals. This allows for contrast to be created between skin and the gunshot residue. The IR photographic documentation should be performed *in situ* prior to preparing the body for autopsy to minimize the loss of any particulate material.

4.2.3 Bruising

IR radiation lightens and smoothes skin tones and is absorbed by blood vessels to appear dark. This can be useful for documenting bruising or patterned injuries on the skin. Figure 4.14 depicts an assault victim who had contusions under the eyes. The IR image of the injuries makes the bruising easier to visualize around the eyes.

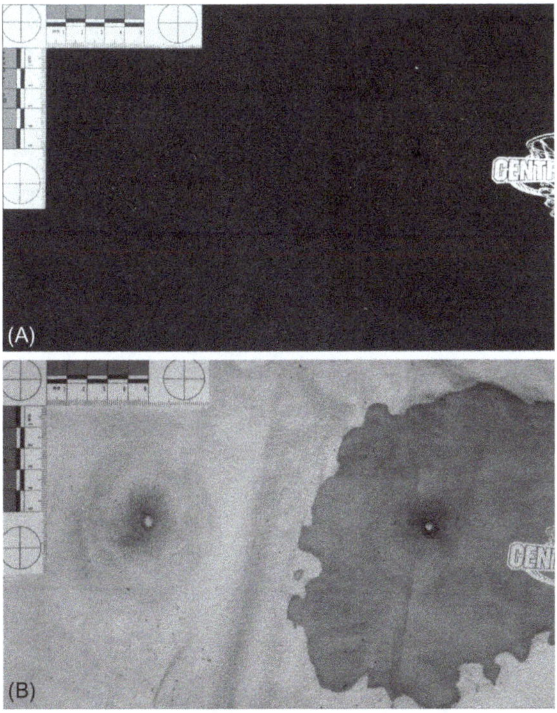

Figure 4.13 (A) Depicts an image of a 100% cotton, black-colored shirt with two bullet entrance holes taken with normal flash photography. (B) An IR image of the same surface. The IR image clearly reveals the bullet holes and corresponding gunshot residue, as well as the saturated bloodstain on the right side of the shirt. The IR image was recorded with a Fuji FinePix S3 Pro with the following exposure settings: f13, *1/60 seconds, ISO 200, flash illumination, Peca 914 (#89B) filter, and operation in aperture priority mode.*

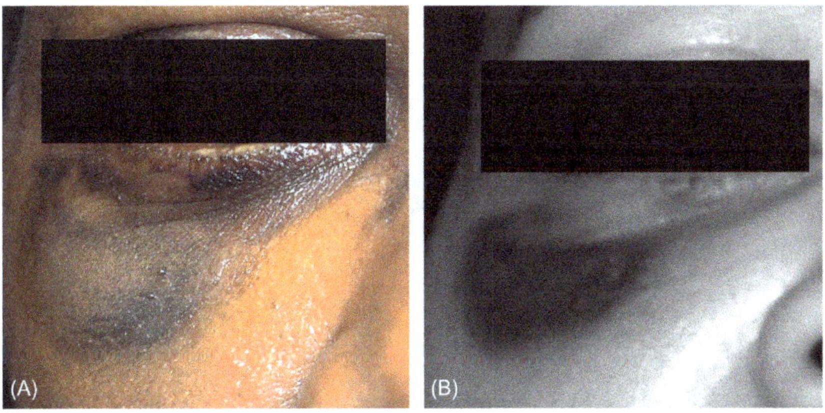

Figure 4.14 (A) Recorded with normal flash photography. (B) Recorded with IR radiation. Note the lightened skin tones and darkened bruising surrounding the eyes. The IR image was recorded with a Fuji FinePix S3 Pro at f9.5, *1/60 seconds, ISO 200, flash illumination, and Peca 912 (#88A) filter.*

4.2.4 Tattoos

Tattoos also appear different in the IR spectrum. Some of the pigments used for tattoos strongly absorb IR radiation and appear dark against the lightened skin. With a properly done tattoo, the dermis layer of the skin is impregnated with the pigment, approximately 1.5–2 mm below the epidermis layer. Tattoos can be a beneficial means to preliminarily identify decomposed or charred remains as long as the dermis layer remains intact. With IR photography, and the dermis intact, visualization of tattoos is possible even if they are not readily visible as in the case with decomposed or charred remains. Figure 4.15 represents images where IR photography was successful in indentifying tattoos on decomposed remains.

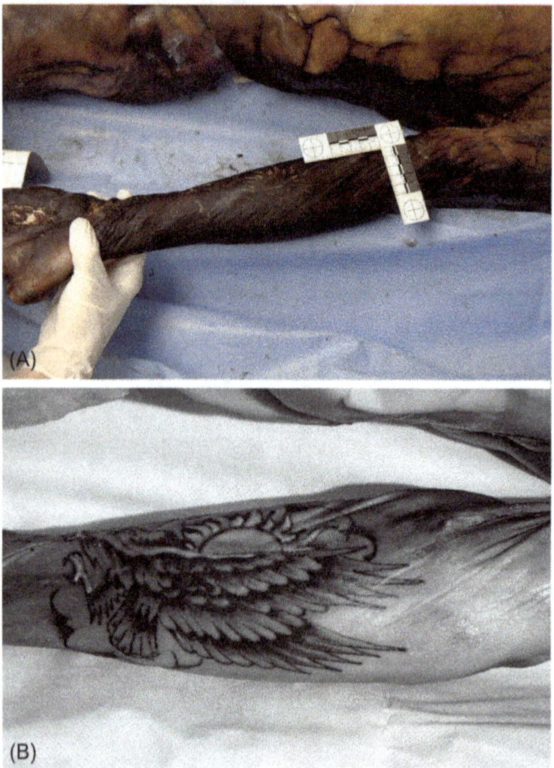

Figure 4.15 In the cases where a deceased is not identified, the documentation of tattoos may be useful. (A) Unidentified deceased whose tissue has undergone decomposition, recorded with normal flash photography. As a result of the decomposition, the details of a tattoo on the deceased's left arm are not clear. (B) IR image recorded with the Fuji FinePix S3 Pro at f8, 1/60 seconds, ISO 200, flash illumination, and a Peca 910 (#87C) filter. As can be seen, the decomposed tissue reflects IR radiation and appears light while the tattoo pigments absorb, thereby creating contrast that reveals the details of the tattoo.

The authors have had the opportunity to photograph living individuals who have undergone laser tattoo removal. After the process is complete and the pigments have been broken down and completely reabsorbed by the body, no indications of the tattoo pigments were identifiable with these individuals using IR photography.

4.2.5 Fingerprint Powders and Dust Impressions

Some fingerprint powders are designed to fluoresce and therefore enhance contrast when they are excited with the proper wavelength radiation. The resulting contrast achieved is a bright image on a relatively dark background. Complementary to this technique is the use of IR radiation to illuminate the fingerprint that has been dusted with black powder or a bichromic powder. These powders can absorb IR radiation and appear dark, while it is likely that a difficult to manage background will lighten up significantly (Figure 4.16).

IR imaging can also be used to reveal dust impressions. This will depend on the physical properties of the dust. Figure 4.17 depicts the patterned, multicolored, 100% polyester fabric. There is a partial footwear impression that had been deposited onto the garment. Figure 4.17A was captured with normal flash photography. Figure 4.17B was recorded with IR radiation using the Fuji FinePix S3 Pro camera. The dust impression was nearly impossible to visualize with the unaided eye. However, in the IR, the multicolored pattern on the shirt is almost completely

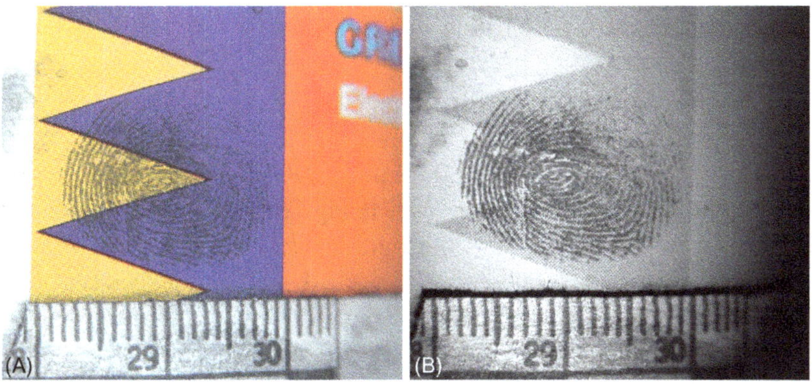

Figure 4.16 (A) A fingerprint deposited on a cylindrical, metal aerosol, container. The fingerprint was developed with cyanoacrylate fuming and dusted with dual-use fingerprint powder. The multicolored background is an ideal surface on which to employ IR photography to better visualize the fingerprint. (B) An IR photograph recorded with a Nikon D100 (unmodified) camera with exposure settings f4.5, 3 seconds, ISO 400, incandescent illumination, and a Kodak Wratten (#87) filter.

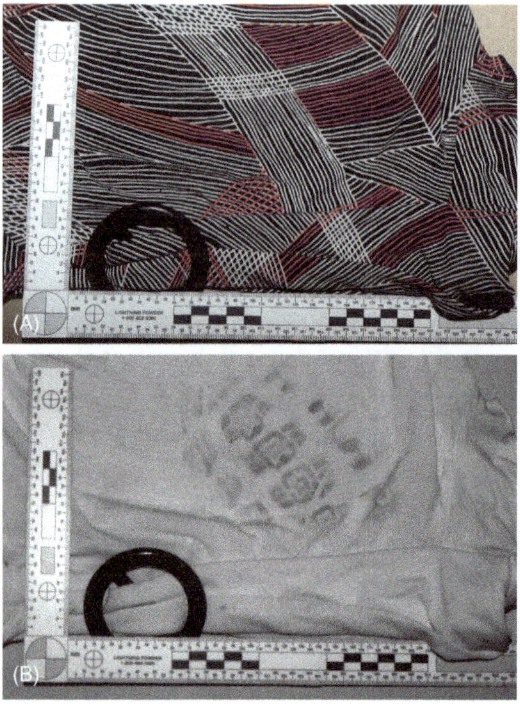

Figure 4.17 (A) Multicolored image of a woman's shirt. (B) IR image reveals the dust impression on the fabric. Recorded with the Fuji FinePix S3 Pro using the following camera exposure settings: f27, 1/60 seconds, ISO 100, flash illumination, and the Peca 914 (#89B) filter.

removed clearly revealing the dust impression. It was determined the dust impression contained mostly carbonaceous soot from stepping through a poorly ventilated, indoor parking structure.

4.2.6 Document Examination

Another useful application of IR photography is for detecting altered documents. With document examination, IR photographic techniques can be used to examine obliterated writing, altered writing, restoration of erasures, and forgeries. IR photography can also be used to visualize charred or faded documents. Inks can be a complex mixture composed of pigments, dyes, solvents, resins, and other materials to make them stable, soluble, and even fluoresce. Two inks that appear visibly identical may absorb, transmit, or reflect IR radiation differently.

In this simple example, two different gel pens were used in the alteration. The black inks appear similar to the unaided eye. However, the inks react quite differently in the IR (Figure 4.18).

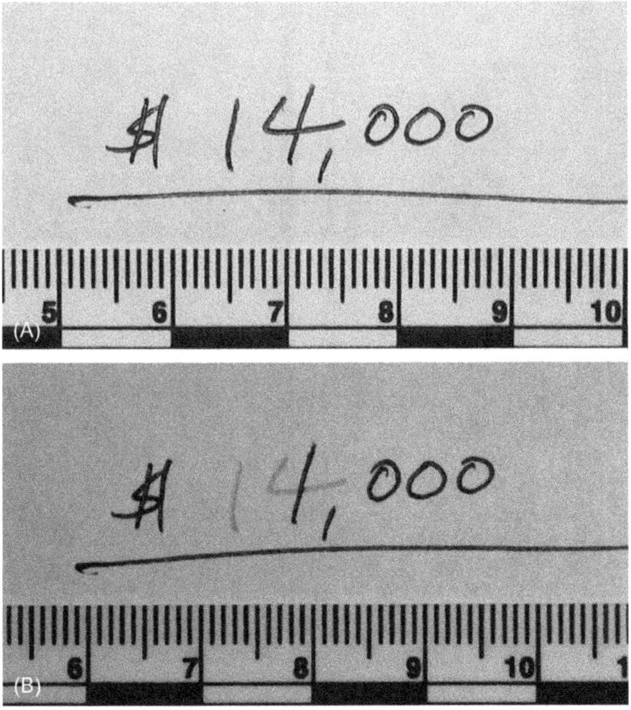

Figure 4.18 Different ink was used to alter the monetary value on this document. (A) Recorded using normal flash photography. (B) IR image recorded with the Fuji FinePix S3 Pro using the following camera settings: f11, 1/250 seconds, ISO 400, flash illumination, and the Peca 914 (#89B) filter.

IR photography can sometimes be used to reveal writing or printing on charred documents. Photographic success with charred documents can vary depending on the amount of charring present. The charred paper can often be lightened with IR radiation. If the ink absorbs IR radiation, it will appear dark with the charred background lightened (Figure 4.19).

US currency and many negotiable banknotes have specially designed security features to act as deterrents against counterfeiting. In this example, a portion of the bank note is printed with green ink that is transparent in the near-IR region. The IR transparent green ink and IR absorbing green ink are designed to be a visual color match under white light illumination (Figure 4.20). When an IR image is examined, the ink appears as lightened stripes on the bills.

4.2.7 IR Luminescence

IR luminescence is a technique where the subject is illuminated, typically with blue light; luminescence is induced where the emission

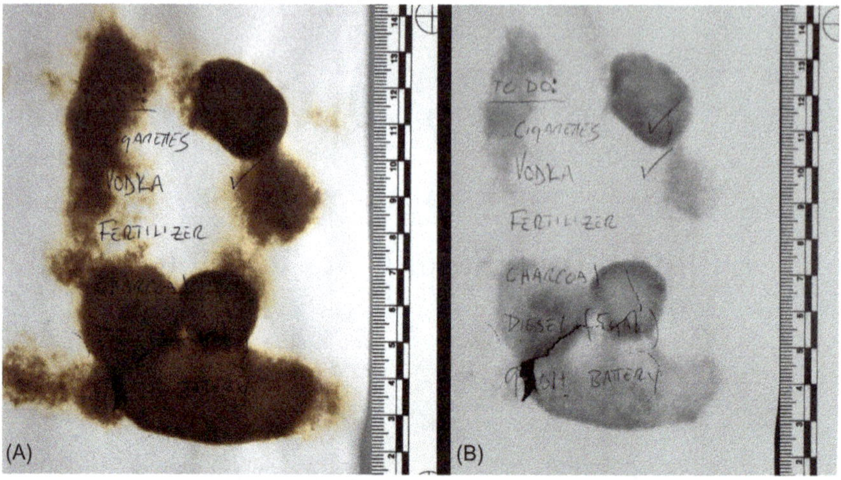

Figure 4.19 (A) A charred document under normal flash photography. (B) The IR photograph that reveals the writing obscured by the charring. The IR image was recorded with a Fuji FinePix S3 Pro at f4.8, 1/250 seconds, and ISO 800, and using incandescent illumination and a Peca 906 (#87A) filter.

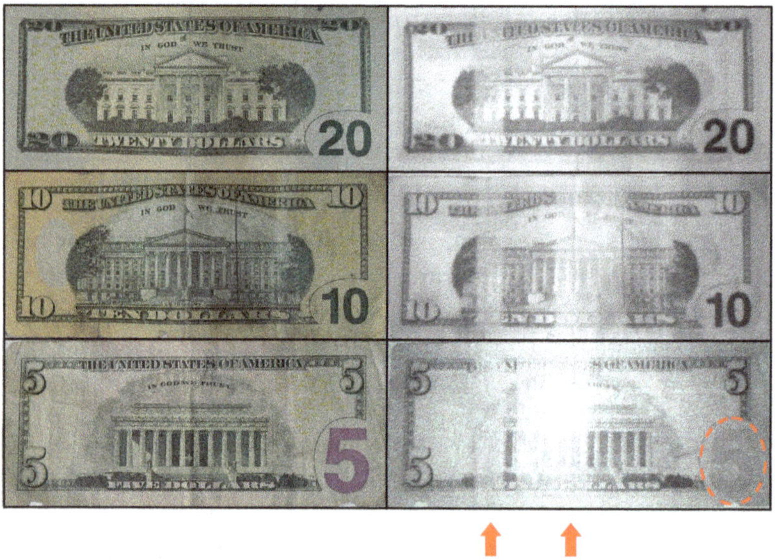

Figure 4.20 IR security markers on several denominations of US currency. Images were captured with a Nikon Coolpix P100 (not modified) camera. The camera settings for the IR images were f5, 1/30 seconds, ISO 160, and flash illumination. The IR filter used was a piece of unexposed but developed Kodak Ektachrome slide film.

occurs in the near-IR. The original technique used a cobalt filter. White light was passed through the cobalt filter (blue in color), which was used to illuminate the subject with light of blue wavelengths. Blue light is higher in energy than IR radiation and can be used to induce

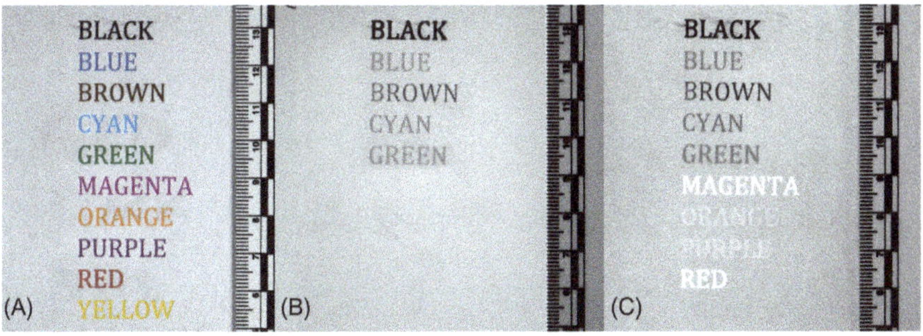

Figure 4.21 IR luminescence of printer inks. (A) Flash photograph. (B) IR image using an incandescent light source and Peca 915 (#89B) filter. (C) IR image using the CSS setting on a Spex CS-16 CrimeScope with a Peca 914 (#89B) filter. All images were captured using a Fuji FinePix S3 Pro camera.

luminescence where the emission can be recorded in the near-IR region. An IR filter is placed over the camera lens that blocks visible light and only transmits IR radiation. Sometimes the technique is referred to as "IR fluorescence", which is not an entirely correct term. Early experimental data demonstrated that in addition to fluorescence, IR phosphorescence might also occur, so the correct term is luminescence.

Using a cobalt filter is not necessary today. The Corning 9788 and the 9780 filters can be used to filter white light. These filters are a blue-green color in appearance and have been used to induce IR luminescence. Using the blue wavebands from a forensic light source can also induce IR luminescence.

In the forensic field, IR luminescence has been used primarily to examine documents. Inks that appear transparent with reflected IR photography may luminesce in the IR using a blue or blue-green band of excitation radiation.

Figure 4.21 shows a sample print of inks from an inkjet printer. The image in Figure 4.21A was recorded with normal flash photography. Figure 4.21B shows an IR image recorded using an incandescent light source and the Peca #89B filter. Some of the inks absorb IR and appear dark, and some appear transparent in the IR region. Figure 4.21C shows an example of IR luminescence. The colors magenta, orange, purple, and red that appeared transparent now luminesce using the CSS setting (broadband blue-green) from the Spex CS-16 CrimeScope and the Peca 914 (#89B) filter.

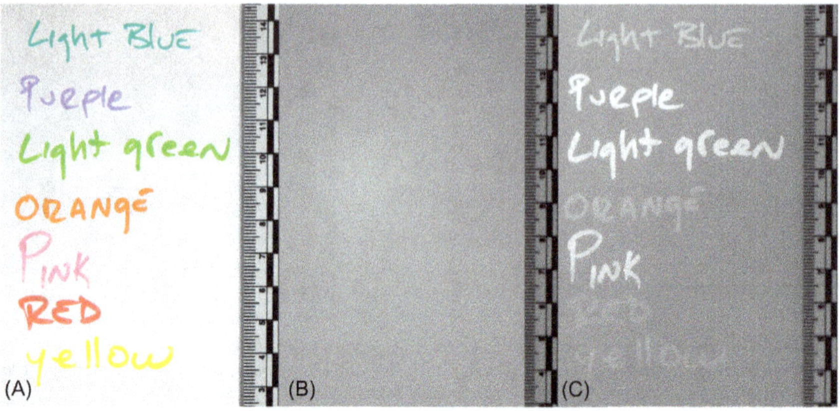

Figure 4.22 IR luminescence of Crayola markers. (A) Flash photograph. (B) IR image using an incandescent light source and a Peca 914 (#89B filter). (C) IR luminescent image recorded with the use of a Spex CS-16 CrimeScope set to CSS with a #89B filter. All IR images were captured using a Fuji FinePix S3 Pro camera.

Figure 4.22 shows sample writing using Crayola brand washable markers. The image in Figure 4.22A was recorded with normal flash photography. Figure 4.22B shows an IR image recorded using an incandescent light source and the Peca 914 (#89B) filter. All of the markers appear transparent in the IR. The image in Figure 4.22C was recorded using the CSS setting from the Spex CS-16 CrimeScope and the Peca 914 #89B filter. All of the colors luminesce to some degree in the IR.

CHAPTER 5

Polarized Light Photography

Polarized light photography is a technique that can be used to increase color saturation, decrease reflections, and increase contrast. The polarized light technique requires two main components, a linear polarizing filter placed in front of an intense white light source and a camera with a polarizing filter placed in front of the lens. With a polarizer in front of the light source and camera lens, the amount of light will be reduced. The exposure compensation will have to be increased by several stops. Caution should be exercised with placing the polarizer in front of a heat-generating light source for an extended period of time. If the polarizer filter gets too hot, it will be irrevocably damaged.

Natural sunlight and most forms of artificial illumination (except lasers) emit light waves that oscillate at all possible angles. Light is considered to be linearly polarized when it contains waves that only oscillate in one direction. A polarizer is a filter that confines the transmission of electromagnetic radiation to one plane. Sheets of polarizing film can be purchased at various scientific supply houses. The polarized film can be cut into various sizes to accommodate different light sources. Polarizers can also be purchased in a fixed, threaded mount to be placed over the camera lens. Polarizers for the camera lens can be a circular polarizer or a linear polarizer. A circular polarizer is a linear polarizer cemented to an optically active (birefringent) material such as quartz. Birefringence is a property exhibited by certain types of crystalline structures that have two or more indices of refraction. The ray of light passing through the material is broken into two unequal waves that travel at different speeds. The light passes through the linear polarizer and becomes polarized. The polarized light next passes through the quartz. When the polarized light passes through a birefringent material, the light ray gets rotated. The light is still vibrating up and down in one plane, but it is now propagating in a corkscrew fashion (Figure 5.1). Some modern digital SLR cameras with autofocus and metering systems may require circular polarizers over the lens. These cameras use beam splitters (partially mirrored surfaces) to reflect light to the viewfinder and the exposure metering system, while

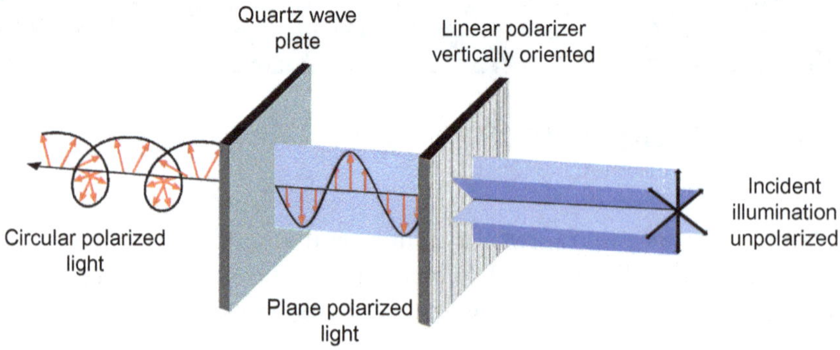

Figure 5.1 The incident beam of unpolarized light is transmitted through a linear polarizer. The linearly polarized light leaving the linear polarizer is transformed into circularly polarized light by a quartz wave plate.

transmitting light to the autofocus sensor. With linearly polarized light, the autofocus and metering systems will not function properly because the beam splitter is dependent on the orientation angle of the linearly polarized light. This is not an issue with circularly polarized light. The beam splitter reflects or transmits circularly polarized light the same way it does for unpolarized light.

Light that is directed onto a sample can be absorbed or reflected. The reflected light can be either a specular or a diffuse reflection. With plane polarized light, the specular reflected light (glare) is essentially still polarized. The plane polarized light impinging the sample that gets diffused can be scattered multiple times; the scattered light that emerges from the sample is essentially random and no longer polarized. Viewing the sample through a linear (or circular) polarizer, which has been illuminated with linearly polarized light, allows the separation of the two components of reflection. Directing the linearly polarized light onto the specimen and viewing the specimen with privileged direction of the polarizers in parallel emphasize the surface features of the sample. With the polarizers positioned in a perpendicular orientation, glare is reduced and the subsurface of the specimen can be viewed (Figure 5.2).

Figure 5.3 illustrates the setup for polarized light photography. The camera should be secured on a tripod or copy stand. To illuminate the sample with plane polarized light, a linear polarizer is placed in front of the light source. The light source should be positioned at a 45–90-degree angle from the subject. It is recommended to reduce

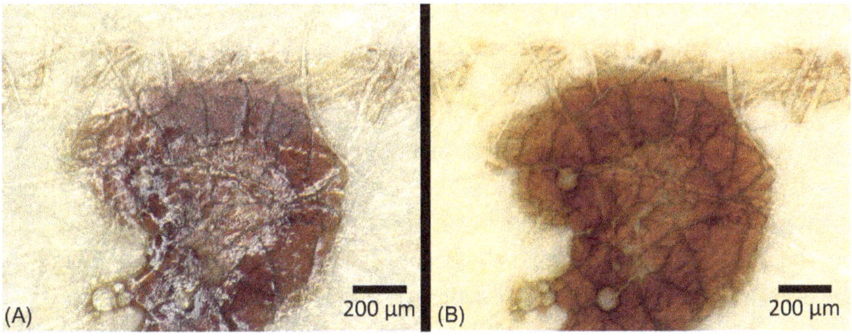

Figure 5.2 (A) Recorded with the privileged direction of the polarizers in parallel orientation. (B) Recorded with the privileged direction of the polarizers in perpendicular orientation. Notable surface features of the bloodstain are visible in (A); with perpendicular polarizers glare is reduced and the fibrous substrate is visible beneath the bloodstain.

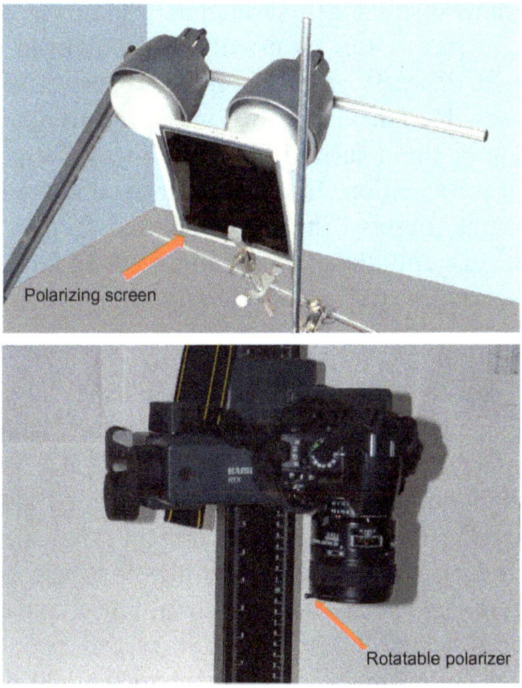

Figure 5.3 A typical setup for photography with polarized light. A polarized filter is placed in front of the light source and a circular polarizer is placed over the camera lens. As polarized light from the light source is reflected from the evidence sample, the photographer must adjust the circular polarizer on the camera lens to eliminate glare from the subject. This procedure should be carried out in a darkened room where the only source of light is polarized. Courtesy of Dr. Peter A. Pizzola.

the ambient light as this light is not polarized and will interfere with the desired effect. A second, rotatable polarized filter is placed over the lens.

Polarizers have a designated privileged direction, which means the direction in which the light waves oscillate after being transmitted through the polarizer. Oftentimes, the privileged direction is indicated on the polarizer. If there is no direction indicated, there are two ways the axis of polarization can be determined. The simplest method is to start with a known polarizer that has a marked axis. Stack the known and unknown polarizer together and transmit light through them. Rotate the unknown polarizer until extinction is achieved, when no light is transmitted. In this orientation, the privileged direction of the unknown polarizer is 90 degrees from the axis of the known polarizer.

Without a known polarizer, the orientation of the unknown can still be determined by observing light that has been reflected from a horizontal, nonmetallic smooth surface at a glancing angle. Specular reflected light, in most cases, is usually well polarized. How well the light is polarized depends on the optical properties of the reflecting surface and the angle of incidence. It is important to note that the direction of vibration of the polarized light will always be perpendicular to the direction of propagation. In order to determine the direction of an unknown polarizer, observe the glare reflected from a shiny surface. Rotate the polarizer until the glare is minimized. In this orientation, the privileged direction of the polarizer will always correspond to the vertical position.

Figure 5.4 depicts a fingerprint on a plastic shopping bag that had been developed by cyanoacrylate fuming and then dusted with a magnetic powder. The area shown in Figure 5.4A was illuminated with a white light-emitting diode (LED) positioned approximately at a 45-degree angle. Substantial glare is present from the reflected incident illumination off the surface of the glossy plastic bag. The image shown in Figure 5.4B was taken with a linear polarizer over the light source and second linear polarizer placed over the lens. The orientation of the polarizer over the camera was 90 degrees perpendicular (crossed polars) to that of the light source. Off-the-shelf polarizers were used to produce this image. The lenses from a cheap pair of polarized sunglasses, purchased from a drugstore, were

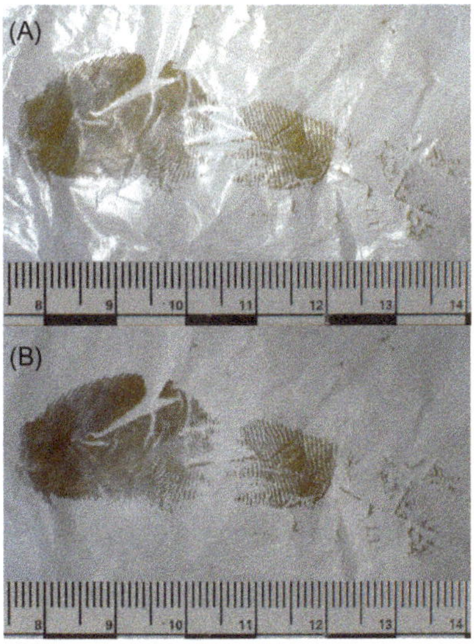

Figure 5.4 (A) Illuminated with a white light LED source. (B) Recorded using polarizers with their respective directions oriented to the perpendicular.

removed from the frame with scissors. The privileged direction of each filter (sunglass lens) was determined by observing the glare reflected from a shiny surface. The polarized lenses were secured over the light source and camera lens with cellophane tape. The photography took place with the aid of a copy stand and in a dark room to eliminate ambient illumination. All the camera settings were the same with the exception of shutter speed. The unpolarized image had a shutter speed of 1/60th of a second. The polarized image had a shutter speed of 1/8th of a second. This equates to a three-stop difference in exposure compensation.

Rotating the polarizer attached to the camera lens allows the user to control the reflected light from the surface of the sample. Removing the entire glare is not always beneficial. Figure 5.5 illustrates an example where specular reflection can help to define certain features of a bloodstain pattern. Figure 5.5 depicts small, circular blood spattering deposited onto a white ceramic floor tile. The spatter had been allowed to completely dry for some period of time. After the stain dried, a light contact transfer was produced over the dried spatter. A contact transfer is a bloodstain pattern produced when a blood covered object come into physical contact with another object or surface. By controlling the specular reflection, the differences can be visualized with respect to

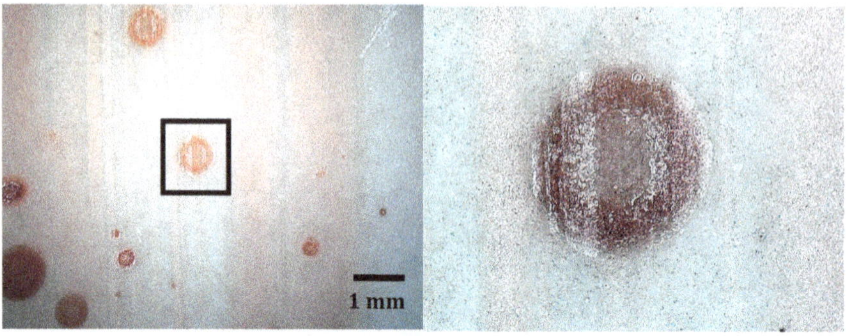

Figure 5.5 In the examination of bloodstain patterns, sequencing overlapping bloodstains can pose a challenge to the examiner. Often, the actual substrate must be physically examined so that techniques utilizing incident and polarized light can be used. These images depict low-pressure contact transfers (streaks) in blood over the top of blood spatters illustrating the continuation of the transfer on the top surface of the stain. The substrate is ceramic tile and the photograph was captured using slightly nonparallel polars.

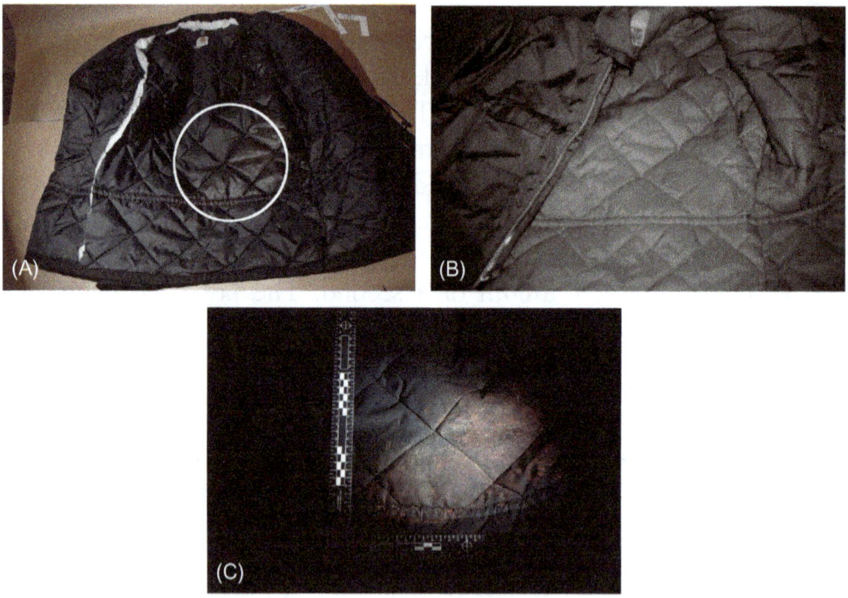

Figure 5.6 The examination of certain garments can pose challenges when attempting conventional photographic documentation methods. (A) Normal flash photography of the inside lining of the jacket fails to adequately establish contrast between the jacket liner and bloodstains. (B) An IR image was captured of the inside lining of the jacket utilizing an incandescent light source and a Fuji S3 Pro UVIR camera fitted with an #89B filter. Unfortunately, the absorbance/reflectance of the liner and blood in the IR spectrum was similar and no contrast was produced. (C) The inside of the jacket liner was additionally photographed with polarized light and a Nikon D80 camera fitted with a 60 mm macro lens and a Nikon circular polarizer. This technique provided the most contrast between the bloodstains and jacket liner. Images Courtesy of Dr. Peter A. Pizzola.

where the contact transfer contacted the top surface of the spatter and were it did not. The polarizers were first set up in a parallel orientation; then the polarizer attached to the camera was rotated slightly off axis to reduce some glare.

Polarized light photography can also be used to enhance contrast and increase the color saturation of certain materials. The following case example illustrates this technique. A black-colored Carhartt jacket was examined for the purpose of bloodstain pattern interpretation. Bloodstains on dark-colored fabric typically pose a challenge to photograph because there is a lack of contrast. Additionally, fabrics such as nylon can have reflective properties that further complicate photographic approaches. Figure 5.6A shows a normal flash photograph of the inside lining of the jacket. Infrared (IR) imaging was attempted with poor results. The fabric reflected much of the IR radiation, negating any potential contrast enhancement between the bloodstains and the fabric (Figure 5.6B). Polarized photography was used to enhance the contrast and color saturation between the dark fabric and the bloodstains (Figure 5.6C).

REFERENCES

Menzel, E.R., 1999. Fingerprint Detection with Lasers, Revised and Expanded, second ed. Marcel Dekker, New York, NY.

Pizzola, P.A., 1998. Improvements in the Detection of Gunshot Residue and Considerations Affecting its Interpretation, PhD Dissertation, City University of New York.

Richards, A., 2010. Reflected Ultraviolet Imaging for Forensics Applications. <http://www.company7.com/library/nikon/Reflected_UV_Imaging_for_Forensics_V2.pdf> [accessed 07.11.12].

Woods, R.W., 1919. Communications secretes au moyen de rayons lumineux. Journal de Physique Theor et Appl. (5th series) 9, 77–90.

www.ingramcontent.com/pod-product-compliance
Lightning Source LLC
LaVergne TN
LVHW021132300926
849160LV00010B/975
* 9 7 8 1 4 5 5 7 7 7 6 2 4 *